To the Ghosts Who Are Still Living

Ami Weintraub

Contents

the ghosts still speak 1
   Releasing the Land 3
   Trees 8
   A Name, A Seed 13
   Silent Rage 17
   Es, Mayn Kinder 23
   Watching the Graves 27
   What We Bury 30
   To my people in the graveyard in Poland 38
   Zingen un Tantsen 40
I still speak 43
   Here, Now 45
   The Mundane and the Holy 49
   Birds with Fire 56
   Why do you stay? 62
   Coiled Potential 67
   Come Back to the Trees 71
but how do I return? 77
   A Sunset Over a Lake 79
   Dancing in Berlin 83
   Lovers, Companions 86
   A clock rings twice a day in the middle of Munich . . . 93
   Almost 94
   The Fruit of Rotting Trees 99
   "Come home" 102
Acknowledgement 107
About the Author 109

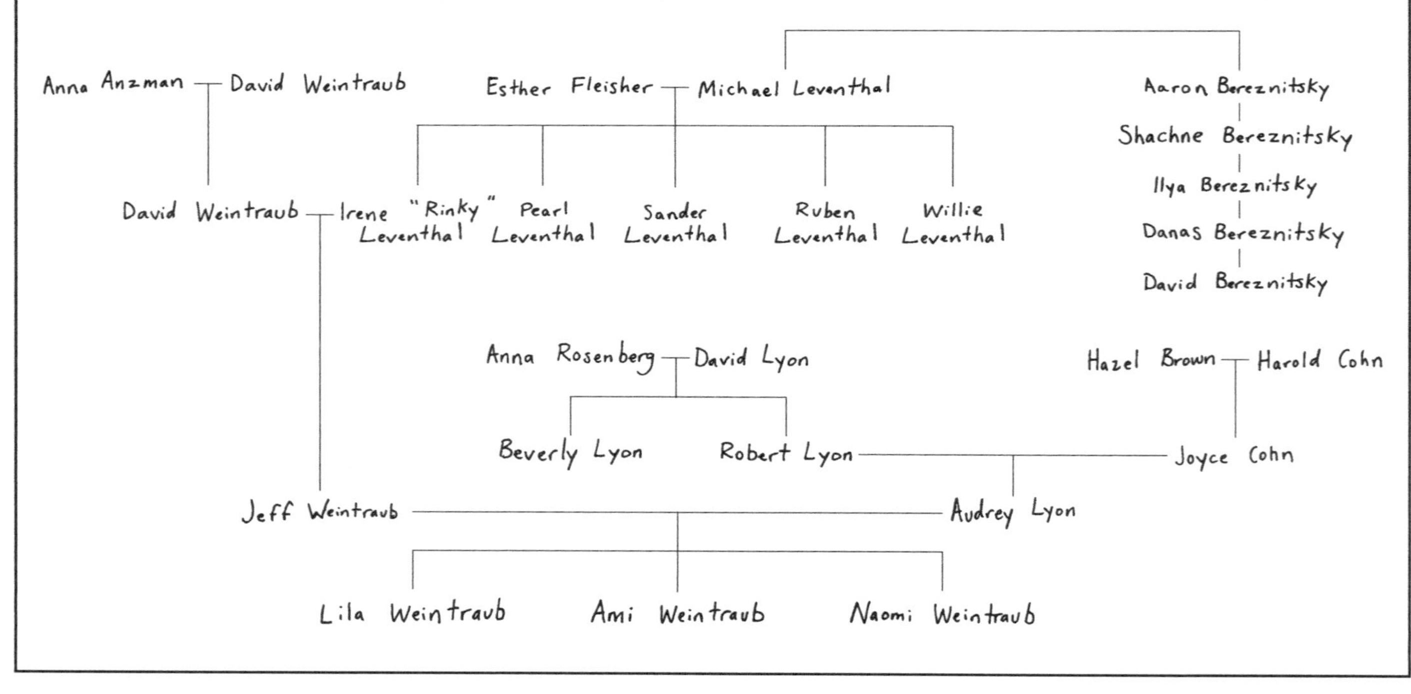

Anna Anzman — David Weintraub
Esther Fleisher — Michael Leventhal
Aaron Bereznitsky
Shachne Bereznitsky
Ilya Bereznitsky
Danas Bereznitsky
David Bereznitsky
David Weintraub — Irene "Rinky" Leventhal
Pearl Leventhal
Sander Leventhal
Ruben Leventhal
Willie Leventhal
Anna Rosenberg — David Lyon
Hazel Brown — Harold Cohn
Beverly Lyon
Robert Lyon
Joyce Cohn
Jeff Weintraub
Audrey Lyon
Lila Weintraub
Ami Weintraub
Naomi Weintraub

The diagram to the left outlines the families in this book, and the following list includes additional descendants omitted from the diagram for the sake of simplicity and because they are not mentioned directly.

Generation 1

Anna Anzman—David Weintraub
    Jerome Weintraub
    Constance Weintraub (Peterson)
    David Weintraub
Esther Fleisher (Leventhal)—Michael Leventhal
    Sander Leventhal
    Pearl Leventhal (Wides) (Roth)
    Jake Leventhal
    Ruben Leventhal
    Willie Leventhal
    Irene "Rinky" Leventhal (Weintraub)
Aaron Bereznitsky (brother of Michael Leventhal)
    Shachne Bereznitsky
      Ilya Bereznitsky
        Danas Bereznitsky
          David Bereznitsky
Anna Rosenberg (Lyon)—David Lyon
    Philip Lyon
    Norman Lyon
    Beverly Lyon (Wolkee)
    Robert Lyon
Hazel Brown (Cohn)—Harold Cohn
    Arnold Cohn
    Robert Cohn
    Joyce Cohn (Lyon

Generation 2
Irene "Rinky" Leventhal (Weintraub) —David Weintraub
    Julie Weintraub (Solomon)
    Jeff Weintraub (my father)
Joyce Cohn (Lyon) - Robert Lyon
    Janet Lyon (Fabiano)
    Audrey Lyon (my mom)
    David Lyon
    Ken Lyon

Generation 3
Audrey Lyon—Jeff Weintraub
    Lila Weintraub
    Ami Weintraub (me)
    Naomi Weintraub

Silver trees sink their roots into the banks of twin lakes. Barely dressed children dive into sloshing waters then rush back to the shade of thin, birch branches. Sun streams through layers of oval leaves, painting yellow and green shadows across dripping, naked bodies. The children crouch and eat blueberries, the trees whisper to the ones who will listen.

"Come home."

the ghosts still speak

Releasing the Land

My great-grandmother's cemetery is now a soccer field. My great-grandfather's synagogue is now a Baptist church. My great-uncle's home is now a police station.

And I live in Pittsburgh, far from these lands where my family no longer exists.

Where are you from?

Behind my great-grandmother's synagogue in Klimentov, Poland was a Jewish graveyard. Humble gravestones marked where my ancestors buried the people they loved.

In the 1900s, pogroms and war and poverty pushed my family from their small town in Poland. My great-grandmother, Anna, was three when her family moved to Argentina, and 12 when they later left for New York. Her parents couldn't afford to take all of their children so they left a young son behind in Poland for his grandparents to raise.

In Argentina Anna ran through the hills with a baby sister and a colorful parrot. In New York she wandered barefoot through the bustling streets, laughing in Yiddish with the women who spoke German.

The family lived in the crowded Lower East Side with the many Jews who had left synagogues and graveyards in lands they hoped would remember them. It was there that Anna gave birth to my grandfather, David.

That was the life they lived, but there was also the death. Anna's baby sister died in Argentina. Her pet parrot was struck by lightning. Her older brother joined them when they moved to New York and screamed like hell for all of the years he had been left behind. While Anna was pregnant with my grandfather, her husband died suddenly. She named my grandfather David after the man he would never meet.

There are so many details I leave behind in this retelling. But I try to remember the joys and the loves she buried in these new lands so far from the small town in southern Poland.

No one told me the name of this place in Poland where my family first lived and died and buried their loved ones. I heard of the town in a letter, written by Anna, tucked into a blue box at the top of my father's closet. It fell off its high shelf one morning when I was rummaging through clothes with my mother.

"Klimentov," written in Anna's handwriting.

There are no more Jews there. I have no more family there.

But I found a fourth cousin online who went back to Klimentov. He taught himself Polish and wandered through the countryside, sneaking into archives and taking pictures of records when the librarian's back was turned. People looked at him funny, and sometimes with fear, when he said he was Jewish. But he continued. After years, he pieced together the marriage dates and birth certificates to make a family tree. Its roots stretch back to the 1700s. We were from there.

We talk on Zoom and he tells me the tales of Klimentov. Centuries ago there was a giant castle outside the city. The royalty built the palace as a perfect oval. Above the living room and dining hall they suspended a giant glass ceiling. They filled it with gallons of water and hundreds of flashing, colorful fish. They ruled the land under a sea of their own creation.

"Were we the kings and the queens?" I ask, dreaming of shadows of sharks and stingrays falling over my dinner plate.

"Of course not," he laughs. But the story lets me imagine a life of fantasy and ease. I remember: I came from a land where beautiful fish swam through the sky.

I am from this place of left-behind boys, man-made oceans, people who fled, cousins who returned.

I am from this place where only a synagogue and a cemetery remember me.

"Home," this sanctuary and burial ground say. "Meet me in the words of the Torah, in the bones of your ancestors. Return to this place."

On September 6, 2018 the Polish government held a ribbon-cutting ceremony atop my family's cemetery. They had just finished building a sports complex, here, on our graveyard in Klimentov.

On the day of the ribbon-cutting ceremony people busied themselves pinning pale yellow and pink balloons onto bright, white goal posts. A man in his 80s wearing a suit and shiny black shoes cleared his throat. With an outstretched arm, he welcomed in a gaggle of children in white dresses and pressed shirts. They gathered around a microphone to give speeches in a language I do not understand. The town's people recounted the dirt they tilled, the basketball hoops they built. They cut a ribbon. They kicked a ball into a goal. They thanked the Polish government who paid $90,000 to make this project possible.

Today, children dribble and shoot and howl with laughter atop my family's bones. They move in the rhythms of their parents. Their dads teach them to pull their foot back and kick the soccer ball as hard as they can. Their parents cheer as the children sprint past. The kids learn what their parents teach them. Their parents teach what their parents taught them.

The children know this is a cemetery for people who no longer live there. They saw the gravestones peeking out of the ground like broken teeth scattered in a dark mouth. They grew up waving to their daddies who sat atop bulldozers, leveling the tombs. After school, the children would sift through the dirt, finding chunks of rocks etched with letters that looked like the bodies of smashed ants. Their moms invited them to build a small white fence around the three remaining gravestones.

"Who's buried here?" the children asked.

But the women didn't hear their question.

On September 6, 2018 the children played on the field they helped their parents build.

These children witnessed the land finally changing hands. With pink balloons and shiny basketball hoops the land that remembers me passed from my ancestors' bodies to the kids wearing white dresses and pressed shirts.

The next generation in Klimentov will only know of my family and this graveyard as a story. They will learn it from the kids who play soccer on a brand new field.

Where am I from?

"Can I even say I am from there?" I ask my fourth cousin. "It's been so long?"

I hear him slam his hands on the table over the phone.

"Do you feel like you are from there?" he asks me.

"Yes."

"Then you are. You are from there, you are from there."

In his words is the hope that our lands won't be lost forever. He still talks about buying the remaining synagogue, turning it into a community center, teaching the kids in Klimentov to be artists and actors. Instead the children learn to play soccer on a brand-new sports field.

Who will tell the story of this small cemetery in southern Poland?

So many have already told me it's been too long, too far. Move on now. Stop remembering, now. Just be like us—they say—the ones who learned how to forget.

I've spent so long teaching myself to remember.

So I write this to the ghosts who are still living with me. You may be the only ones who believe this story. We tell it together.

You: creating my body from all that you lived through.

Me: writing down the memories you share.

I want the land to remember me and tell our story. Until then, I turn these words into a mirror so we can behold ourselves more clearly.

My great-grandmother's synagogue still stands next to the new sports complex. It is a large white building with a triangle roof and steep steps that lead to its front door. My fourth cousin tells me about a man who sneaks into the building to sell my great-grandma's candlesticks to tourists. He stands on the steps of the temple, throws off the broken lock on the front door and wanders into the empty sanctuary. He looks for the menorahs my great-grandmother lit with her mother, the yad her father used to read Torah.

Treasures for me and for him.

I imagine prayer books tucked neatly in the backs of each seat, or maybe they are strewn in a corner under the crumbling ceiling. Their pages are dogeared and words underlined. I'm coming right back, they seem to say. Wait here a while.

The man grabs the siddurim in his thick fingers; dust flies into the air and he coughs as he opens the molded over covers. In one version of this imagining, the prayer books have been sitting in the backs of each seat for decades, ready for a minyan to pick up where they left off. In another, they have been covered in rubble waiting for someone to find them.

He laughs at the mangled black letters lining the pages. They look like smashed ants, dying over and over in new formations.

Treasures for me and for him.

He arranges the objects he collects in the front room of his house. He calls it a museum. Tourists turn the items over in their hands, running their fingers along the ornate decorations. They smile at the beautiful things and pay him 10 zlote, 20 zlote for the menorahs, the yads, the prayer books.

This is how they remember us.

They pack the remains of my family into their bags.

The children play. The man makes a living.

The destruction is still happening.

In present tense.

I wake up from a dream and hear your wailing.

You remember the people who pried our fingers from the grounds that know us.

But how do I return?

When I live in Pittsburgh, far from these lands where my family no longer exists.

Where are you from?

Trees

Based on the true story of my great-grandfather's brother.

And now we write to you:

We were gone for so long. But it was only four years—it just felt like so long because our bodies became so thin, our families so lost.

I was tired. So tired. And they opened the gates of the camp and I ran in the direction of home.

I saw the birch trees. First a dotting of papery trunks by the road, then the occasional sighting turned into a grove, and finally a forest of white branches. The trees whispered to me, singing songs they had taught us in Vishay, the village where I grew up. Old friends, loving family—there if only you know how to listen.

I slept at their roots as I slowly made my way through the Lithuanian countryside. At night their branches opened, just a bit, so I could see the expanse of stars. Four years and nothing had changed.

I dreamt of my mother, her hands rolling dough, plucking feathers, mending clothes—reaching towards me, pulling me close. I dreamt of the tree frogs croaking by the twin lakes. The expanse of water sent creeks rambling through the forest like veins in a body.

I dreamt while I slept and while I walked. The promise of home pushed me onward. Only four years—what could have changed?

I cried and the trees sheltered me. They offered me food and covered my body with branches. They listened to me shriek.

The solitude on the journey was a comfort after being crammed into such small spaces with dying, diseased bodies. I wailed when I thought of the thin arms and legs forced to labor next to me. I looked down at myself and saw my thin arms, my thin legs. I remembered pulling heavy stones from the ground while the guards yelled at us like we were prisoners. We were prisoners.

"We'll take your stories for you," I could hear the trees saying. "Let us have it, let us take it. We are old and our roots stretch deep into the earth. The pain has more space in our bodies, more ways to leave. We won't be burdened by it."

I imagined wrapping my stories in brown paper, tying them with a messy bow, and handing the trees parcel after parcel of these heavy packages. Only four years but so many stories. I thought of my words moving down through their roots, into the deep expanse of earth. The trees would sigh and release my pain into the soil, to decompose next to dead leaves and old fossils—to create ground for new forests to grow.

That's how I wandered away from the camp. Back through time to four years before—my mom with the chickens, the lakes with their creeks. The world I knew, coming nearer with each step forward.

One day I came to the edge of the forest. The trees were laughing and singing me their songs. I was caught in their delight, I hardly noticed the murky smell of the lake, the babbling of the rushing creeks. Home.

I stood with my hand on the trunk of a swaying birch, staring out at the grass that separated the trees from the sleepy houses and roads.

"I'm back," the words caught in my throat. I wanted to rush through the town to find my mother with her arms opened wide.

But it had been four years. I stepped back and felt the trees tremble with the stories I had told them. I didn't want to leave the forest.

"Go!" I heard them whisper.

So I walked out of the patch of trees.

My feet carried me down the familiar paths. I walked up the gravel streets, past the church, by the shops. Just as I'd done four years ago. But there were no men rushing by to daven, no children chanting songs at cheder. Quiet. I could hear the frogs on the lake chirping louder than I ever had.

As the sun set I wandered through the town. I looked back at the forest and silently begged the trees to take me in again. I longed for the starry journey, where home was still a dream.

The truth of what remained was not surprising. I'd talked to the men who came into the camp. They would recount which village they were from, how many Jews had been taken, how many survived the trains. Counting up the towns and the numbers of people I knew they had collected nearly all of us. There were the Rabbis of Villnius, the peddlers of Grodno, the liars and the thieves and the saints all gathered into one horrible Ghenna. My beautiful Jewish family; together one last time.

But I still dreamed; if I had survived maybe my mother, my wife, my daughters had, too.

Finally my feet let me stop. I looked up and saw I was in front of the home I had helped build with my father and brother; the home where my wife and children lived while I went away a long time ago to peddle in a nearby town. I was gone for four years then. Four years and not much had changed. My daughters grew a bit taller, their hair became long enough to tie back into pretty braids. But not much had changed in those four years, long ago.

I held the door knob in my tired palm. I felt the familiar grooves and ridges of the handle, it was the one I had made in my blacksmith shop and affixed to this door when my father and I built this house. I had carved two little birds in the mold. In their beaks, they brought curved branches together to make a heart, blooming with leaves. The birds with their branches reminded my wife of my love for her whenever she entered our home.

I turned the knob but it wouldn't budge. It was locked. I looked down at my hands as if I might still have a key after all of these years.

"A man without a key to his own house." I laughed at this most minute example of my misfortune. It was a minor hindrance when I could almost feel the warm stove inside and imagine the sleeping loft in the attic getting toasty. All of the aches in my body throbbed with a deeper need, knowing they would soon be cared for,

I raised my hand and knocked, sending an echo through the quiet town. Someone shuffled on the other side of the door. I grinned wide, my dry lips cracking. I opened my arms, readying myself to catch my daughters as I used to do when I would come home.

When the door opened, a tall man with a thick mustache and bulging muscles stepped out. He wore a dark blue uniform with golden buttons on the coat and lapel. His hat was blue with a red stripe encircling it, a flat brim cast a shadow over his eyes.

Drunk on the sight of my home, I hardly thought anything of this strange man standing in the doorway. I tried to look around him, to see if my wife was reading or my daughters were playing with the dolls I'd bought them. Maybe my mother was cooking lokshen soup for my homecoming. But in the dull glow of the kerosene lamp burning inside, I only saw more men who looked like the one in the doorway. Thick mustaches, blue uniforms, muscles that bulged like mine had before men like these had taken me away.

Where was my mother?

My voice trembled as I looked up at the man in my doorway.

"Excuse me sir, this is my home," I said.

Nothing changed about his demeanor except a slight twitch in his lip. The tremor betrayed his fear; he was scared of this ghost of a man who had returned to claim what was his. The chatter of the men behind him quieted. The chirps of the frogs grew louder.

The man adjusted the bottom of his jacket and regained his composure.

"This home," he said in a Lithuanian accent I hadn't heard in years. "It's a police station now."

I stared back at him and saw the dream of my wife, my daughters, my mother fade into shrieks and terror.

"There is nothing left for you here."

"No! No!"

I screamed like an animal unleashed from a cage. I lunged at the man, frantic, trying to grab hold of what was mine.

He slammed the door in my face.

"It's my home!"

I banged against the door I had built with my father. I shook the locked door knob so hard the little birds cut my palms.

I wailed and the police officers carried on with their evening. I could smell their cigar smoke wafting out from the kitchen window. They laughed and spoke in a hushed tone.

The blood from my hands stained the doorposts.

I was a man at the door of his house without a key. Four years and there was nothing left for me here.

I staggered to the birch trees. My eyes were red circles of tears, my arms reached out for the embrace of their trunks. My throat was so raw I could no longer scream the curses I had for the police who had stolen my home from me.

"Take me home!" I called to the birches. And they opened their branches and took me in.

Hey, hey, Daloy Polizei
Means the same thing now as yesterday.
Out of your houses, into the streets,
Everybody say, "Fuck the police!"

—Geoff Berner
Based on the Yiddish Folk Song "Daloy Politsey"

A Name, A Seed

I found a long-lost cousin after talking to my great-uncle Willy.

"Our last name was Bereznitzky," Willy told me a year before he passed away. "But they changed it to Leventhal when they got here."

Bereznitsky. A name we lost long ago.

I hum the word between my lips, drawing out the "zzzzzz" and the "kyyyy," so I sound like I am singing these strange sounds, detached from living people, only reviving themselves in the stumbling movements of my clumsy tongue.

We didn't know that anyone with this name was still alive.

The last time I saw my grandma Rinky I pushed her in her wheelchair at my cousin's wedding. Long ago, her parents' Russian pronunciation of her name turned, "Irene," into, "Irinka," into, "Rinky." I'd never known her any other way.

I settled my grandma next to a plate of salmon and broccoli at the hotel reception table. I broke the food into small pieces for her to eat.

"I'm learning Russian this year in college," I told her.

She stared at me, hand-drawn eyebrows raised and her red-painted lips parting incredulously.

"Why would you do that? There's no reason to learn that," she drawled.

"Because of you, because your family spoke it."

I was the first generation to never hear the accent of an old country voice. I wanted to feel the words her parents spoke in my own mouth.

My great-grandfather, Michael, came to the US escaping the Russian military conscription in the early 20th century. At the time, the army drafted Jewish men and boys for upwards of 20 years.

Officials would come to Jewish towns and take boys from their families, shackling them in chains and paying high sums for kidnappers to steal them.

After 20 years in the army, the government hoped the men would either die in battle or become fully assimilated into Russian culture, forgetting the communities they left long ago. Some of my great-grandfather's cousins had already been conscripted, occasionally sending home stories of their humiliation: the Russians forced them to eat molded, unkosher food and they forbade them even as soldiers from carrying guns because they were Jewish. So, as everyone says, my great-grandfather left out the back door as the Russian army knocked on the front door. He fled with his brother and eventually settled in Indianapolis where he became a car wrecker. He was scared the Russian army would find him in this new land so he changed his name from Bereznitsky to Leventhal.

"Don't bother with learning Russian," Grandma Rinky's eyes trembled behind the fog of old age while she stabbed at the pale salmon on her plate. I brushed my hand through the thinning curls on her head.

Irinka, Rinky. This language was part of her name. But even at the end of her life, she felt it was still too unsafe to speak it. Like pronouncing the sounds might act like a spell: conjuring the banging of a fist on a door, the shoving of hands against bodies, the clattering of chains. The past still lived in our fear.

Bereznitsky.

I typed it into Facebook one day, hoping to find a living person attached to the name.

Outlined in the dark blue Facebook logo, was a man with this same collection of harsh consonants trailing his first name. Danas Bereznitsky. He was from Lithuania, in his 30s; an artist who drew eccentric animations. He was already friends with my great-uncle Willy on Facebook.

I messaged him.

"We might be related, my great-grandfather changed his name from Bereznitzy to Leventhal," I typed.

"Yes!" he replied. "It's me."

It's me. I repeated it out loud. The name was alive.

I laughed at the simple joy of seeing a word I knew written by another person. "Bereznitsky" on the lips of a stranger who is now my cousin.

"Both names mean birch tree," my new cousin told me. "One in Lithuanian, one in Hebrew." This tree that grew in my great-grandparent's village was helping us find each other once again. My body trembled. I felt the banging of fists on a door, the shoving of hands against bodies, the clattering of chains. The old fear filled me.

But now I knew these horrors were over.

For so long I'd been holding the fear of children stolen from parents and families turned to ashes. I never learned the end of the story of this distant land I was not supposed to speak of. One piece of our family survived: There was a man who was alive and he was an artist with wiry drawings. He returns to our village to fish in the summers. He was safe. We were safe now.

So many years later my body finally learned the terror was over.

My cousin and I talked online and made plans for him to meet the Leventhals. Months later, 40 of my dad's cousins gathered on Zoom. It was a big family reunion; online, because of the pandemic, but we were there.

My aunt cried when my dad asked her to introduce herself. Cousins wiped away tears as they said hello. No one explained why they were crying, but so much had changed since we had last been together. There was the new absence of Willy and Rinky; the long ago passing of their brothers Sander, Ruben, and Jake. And then there was the presence of the cousins we hadn't known were alive. People turned ghosts, ghosts turned people.

An old man who had grown up in Lithuania stared wide-eyed into the camera.

"There are so many of you," he said, silently scanning each of our tiny, virtual faces. "I don't know what to say. All I can do is smile."

"There's so many of you," I thought with a shared disbelief.

We were branches of a family tree, long separated. Both sides thought they were the only ones left. We were the cousins who had moved far, far away. They were the cousins who had stayed in Lithuania during a brutal war. We were ghosts to each other. But now we watched a newborn with red hair squirm in my Ohio cousin's arms. We laughed at the joyful way my Lithuanian cousin teased his father.

The banging of a fist on a door, the shoving of hands against bodies, the clattering of chains. It was over.

Here we were: living, breathing people.

Silent Rage

Dear Ben,

A lot has happened since you first asked me to tell this story of hope or truth or rage. It was a story to me then. Something I could imagine in adventure-movie style; flames of glory surrounding our friends as we fought back against evil.

Now I feel it for myself. I have memories now, Ben. Memories of events I didn't live through. But memories that have always somehow been mine.

Before I remembered, I thought colonization functioned differently for Jewish people. Like maybe this theory that antisemitism is such a unique form of oppression meant we actually hurt less. We were somehow different from other people who have also felt pain as a people.

But I've been wanting to tell you this memory of my family. It makes everything feel simultaneously more simple and more awful. I've known its outline my whole life, like it was a dream I had when I was a child. And I think you might know it, too.

It starts with a hand-drawn map of Vishay, Lithuania. I learned the name of this village from the football team my grandfather jokingly raved about.

"Your great-grandfather and all of his brothers played for the Vishay Bulldogs," he'd tell me when I was young.

He loved to tell stories like this about the family he'd married into. His own father died while his mother was pregnant with him. His siblings scattered throughout the country after they served in World War II.

My grandmother came from a swarm of loud brothers, loyal sisters, and joyful parents who traveled the world to stay together. I could tell my grandfather was looking for a family like this. For stories that would nurture him through the loss of a man he never met.

I think we are searching for something similar, my grandfather and me. So I call out to him now in the only way I know how.

"Ya'amo David Weintraub HaCohain Ben David Weintraub HaCohain." And I patiently wait for him to return my call.

Once we began speaking again, we couldn't stop. He showed up in my dreams, at the bus stop, while I was eating with friends. He led me to this memory and helped me understand its power..

So, this map of Vishay. I found it on a website called—you won't believe it—but it's called Shtetllinks.com. It's a barely functioning holdover from the dot-com era that gave me as close to a feeling of opening a dusty, ancient box that I can still get.

A man named Yosif Levinson had drawn out a bare-bones map of Vishay, the village my father's maternal grandparents came from. This map maker lined the one main road and two giant lakes with small squares labeled "Jewish Houses." Each house had a number and each number was assigned to a family. This man, Yosif Levinson, knew where every Jew lived—like you might remember the homes of your closest friends.

So there it was. Simple. "66. Bereznitsky" down by the bend in the road. "62. V. Fleisher" right next to the synagogue and the lake. My great-grandparents grew up only numbers apart from each other. I could feel their love story stretching out between these houses like giddily hung streamers.

Seeing that little square next to the water helped me remember the gurgling sound of tides breaking under the weight of oars. There was my family with bulging muscles and gritted teeth casting out coarse, handmade nets. There they were, catching fish in the light of early dawn to later sell at market.

And the synagogue. It, too, nestled along the banks. When we sat in the pews the beautiful smell of clean water and earthy mud wafted through the windows. We breathed its scent into our lungs as we gathered under the wooden shelter to honor every blessing and curse that befell us.

This is my family's story. The part that's easy to write about. The Before heals me more than knowing the details of After. But every Jewish family has some story of After that is easier to tell if we didn't know what came Before.

After is choppy, ugly. But I need to share it with you. Still, admitting to it makes me feel embarrassed. Like I'm asking for your pity. Like you haven't felt this sorrow, too.

But I feel its weight hanging heavy on my bones.

When I was 19 I drunkenly clung to a toilet, nauseous, crying for hours in a visceral awakening to our pain. I shouted to the strangers at the party, "Can you believe this happened? Can you believe this happened?"

I asked because I was embarrassed to feel so alone.

The story continues like this: members of my family immigrated to the US around the 1920s. They became car wreckers in Indianapolis, and had children who had children who gave birth to me.

But Vishay still stood. There were brothers and parents and kids walking to synagogue, falling in love, catching fish in this town cut in two by its lakes.

I learn the rest from Google searches.

On June 2, 1941 the German army invaded Vishay. With the help of local Lithuanians they forced all of the remaining Jewish men into the synagogue. At night they locked up the doors and windows. During the day they sent the men out to do humiliating manual labor like cleaning the streets and destroying Soviet bunkers.

By September 15, 1941 the Germans took all of the remaining Jews of Vishay to a nearby ghetto on the Katkiškės estate where they lived until November 3rd.

There's a video on YouTube channel titled "Prayer Meeting Veisiejai" that was posted in 2017. You should look it up if you're curious. In the video two men walk arm in arm down a long, wooded path. The trees are so green and dark and lush I thought it was a CGI background.

"So you became a Christian in 1991," the man behind the camera asks in a TV host voice.

"Yes, about 23 years ago," says the man in what I assume to be a Lithuanian accent.

"And now we are going to a prayer meeting!" the loud voice behind the camera announces as if he is narrating migrating salmon in a wildlife video.

The camera cuts to a boy playing piano in a big wooden room.

And it cuts to three people standing outside a simple, lime-green building.

"This is our church right here!" Again, the man behind the camera.

He zooms in on a gold plaque hung on the outside wall. It lists the name of the church and its website.

"This is the site of an old Jewish synagogue," the accented voice says from off screen.

"This is awesome!" says the man behind the camera.

And then we all walk into the Baptist Church that was once my family's synagogue.

The video is so slow and deliberate. I can see everything. The doorway where the mezuzah was once affixed, the wide hallway where little kids played hand games while waiting for their parents to stop schmoozing. The doors that were once barred shut every night.

Then the Christian people singing hymns in the pews. Laughing and holding yellow flowers. A giant cross hanging in front of the big windows. The breeze blowing the curtains, letting in that beautiful smelling air.

I study their faces to see if they look anything like mine.

I call my great uncle a week after watching the video. We speak for the first time since my grandmother died.

I want to ask him what he remembers. He starts simply, "It was very hard for them."

He uses words that are still urgent 100 years later. My father escaped the Russians. My mother and older brother ran from house to house, hiding behind stoves. On the boat, she was scared they'd be turned back because my brother had a cold.

He sends me a packet of documents. Photos of my great-grandmother Esther and her boy Sander at Ellis Island. Pictures of an awkward child dressed in a Soviet button-up next to a man with a beat-up jacket and flowing white beard. A woman with gaunt cheeks and a babushka covering her hair.

There's a recent picture of a yellow house with a red tin roof overlooking a lake. Three people stand at the locked door, hand on the door knob. Number 62.

In 2004 my grandmother's cousin Rochelle wrote in an email, "The yellow house is the one Velvel lived in as a fisherman—on the lake. Esther and Sander lived there until they came to the US. My uncle (he is 89 right now) is in a lawsuit trying to get the property back—lakefront after all."

I hope this story speaks for itself. I am only 23 but I have already spent years trying to recall what we have lost.

I know we speak so much about the After but it's the Before that I want to try and remember. The Yiddish songs Esther sang as she made Shabbos chicken and stinky's smeltz. The wet stones glowing on flames, steaming up the hot houses where people took a shvitz.

But it's harder for my great uncle to recall these things. Instead he tells me about being so poor in America they couldn't afford a second set of dishes for Pesach. My aunt tells me they couldn't keep Kosher because there were few Kosher butchers in a city like Indianapolis.

We are living in the After that our grandparents taught us to call paradise. But we know they never felt fully comfortable here either. They told us to be grateful our neighbors accepted us. But the lauded safety always felt contingent on our ability to prove our gratitude with assimilation. They tried to teach us as much about Before as they could without crying.

Now, I'm hardly a grandchild anymore. My grandparents whisper their memories into my ears while I sleep. And I have my own memories now. I remember my dad affixing his kippah only when we pulled into the parking lot of our synagogue. I remember my mom asking my best friend not to gloat about what she did on Saturdays because I was at synagogue and felt left out. My friend's mother yelled at my mom that night and canceled our sleepover.

I remember more horrors I couldn't hide from the six-year-olds I teach in Pittsburgh. They lived through the terrors. And now their own memories make them fear themselves.

I yearn for the synagogue, the yellow house, the lake. I'm angry they took it from us, Ben. I'm angry they are forcing us to fight a perpetual war as consolation.

I'm angry they made us forget.

And this is all I can remember.

Love and RAYJ,

Ami

הכרבל ונורכיז

Zikhronah Livrakha

May their memory be a blessing

Es, Mayn Kinder

My mother's grandmother, Anna, came from the town of Alexandrovsky in Russia. I searched for the name of this town on Google and Wikipedia, but there were so many towns with the name Alexandrovsky I couldn't tell exactly which one my family was from.

Somewhere in the taiga of Irkutsk or on the mountainous shores of the White Sea, Anna spent her childhood collecting eggs from chickens, or maybe baking bread with her mother in their home's small kitchen, or perhaps gathering children around her and telling them long stories of the monsters and fairies who ran through her shtetl's mysterious forests.

"She was always a smart woman, a clever woman," her daughter, Beverley, tells me over the phone. Beverley is in her 90s now, but she remembers how her mom would help brew cherry wine in the basement of her family's Chicago apartment. Throughout Beverley's childhood there were huge vats of alcohols and fruit compotes gurgling in the cold depths of their West Side building.

Beverley tells me about the piroshkis Anna cooked. The fried hand pies were so tempting, my young grandfather and the little boys in the building would steal them hot off the baking pan when Anna's back was turned. Seemingly tired of their thievery, one day Anna filled the meat-stuffed treats with spoonfuls of egg shells instead. When the boys grabbed the piroshkis from the trays and bit down, they covered their mouths in disgust and surprise as thin, hard shards crushed between their teeth.

"They never stole the piroshkis after that," I could hear Beverly smile at the memory of her mother pulling such a prank on my five year-old grandfather.

I was on the phone with Beverly at the beginning of the pandemic. I was trying to learn how to make it through the uncertainty of a world of illness, job losses, and the threat of food shortages. I was learning that cherry wine could be brewed in a basement, and there was a hand pie with an odd name that my grandfather loved so much he would steal it while it was piping hot.

No one had told me about these ways my family had eaten. These foods didn't show up on the Forward's nearly monthly list of "Classic Jewish Dishes," that always exalted the latke and the bagel. We were silent about so much that had kept us alive for so long.

"Let me feed you," I heard Anna whisper into my ear as I nervously opened the cupboard in my small kitchen in Pittsburgh. I felt her guide me to the recipe for the Russian piroshkis and grasp my hands so I would knead the dough with more strength.

"Heat up the oil and fry them until they are crisp and puffy," the recipe told me as Anna watched the oil pop on my stove. I dropped the circular buns into the oil and they crackled and sputtered, spitting out small bubbles of liquid. One by one I pulled them out with a slotted spoon and rested them on a blue plate covered in a thick paper towel.

After they cooled I held the finished golden pastry in my hand. The filling of ground beef mixed with rice and parsley was bursting out of the seams of the buns. They didn't look like the perfect, uniform treats I saw in the recipes online. They had puffed into an array of oddly shaped semi-circles. But still, I held the finished golden pastry in my hand.

"Nu? Est mein kinder." Eat my child. Anna and her mother and her mother nudged my hand as they poured themselves sloshing glasses of cherry wine.

July 2020 was the first time I was able to go home to see my parents and siblings during the pandemic. My family hugged one another, and held hands and faces, and gave haircuts; and they took walks around the block to see how the trees had already bloomed, but the gardens were still growing colorful with summertime flowers; and the neighbor kids were getting taller—have you seen how tall they are?—and they're almost about to graduate from high school; and there's talk that the elementary school is going to be torn down, we should really walk by and see it before it's gone.

We sat on the porch and watched the summer float past. We missed each other.

On a sun filled afternoon, I pulled my mom and siblings into the kitchen.

"We're going to make piroshkies," I told them. I took the flour and oil and rice from the pantry and measured them out on the counter. I showed my sibling and sister how to knead the dough with strength, how to put the right amount of beef and rice in the center and fold the edges of the pastry so the filling was wrapped like a gift.

And we fought: How much garlic should go in the ground beef, and maybe we should try a new shape for the buns, or roll it out a bit thinner, no thicker, no thinner. The yelling would overtake the kitchen and then break out into laughter and then more quipping. We had missed each other.

As the buns fried, my mom shook her head.

"I can't believe we are cooking food my grandmother made." I waited for my mother's nostalgic memories of her beloved grandmother. "Grandma Anna was such a bad cook!"

All of her siblings had agreed that their grandmother had been terrible at baking. She'd bring out shortbread that was missing butter, sugar cookies that were missing sugar, chocolate cake that never had enough chocolate.

"She was always forgetting the parts of the desserts that actually made it taste good," my mom laughed as she told me how Anna would bring them into the kitchen, pull hairnets on their heads and teach them to cook these onslaughts of terrible pastries.

Anna had learned to cook as her family was in the midst of job losses, food shortages, illness, and violence. She watched her family abandon the gurgling vats of cherry wine that brewed in the cellars of Alexandrovsky. They had decided to pack up and leave Russia after a final pogrom tore through the shtetl. She was nine years old and already in a routine of closing the wooden shutters of her house when pogroms rang out on the Jewish street.

Her dad left first, allegedly traveling through China to get to America. There was family already in Chicago who had built a mutual aid group known as the Pinkus Rosenberg Society. They raised money to help other family members leave Russia and settle in Chicago's Jewish West Side.

I wondered what food Anna took on the ship to America. I imagined the piroshkis sliding into her pockets, warming her hands. The seemingly perfect food for a hard journey. But she would not have been able to bring enough pies to last the amount of time they were in steerage. The ship jostled them and threw them about as they barreled along the sea, the nausea and the putrid smells growing with each day. Those weeks on the ship were so bad that 50 years later Anna nearly refused to get on a tourist ferry in downtown Chicago which Beverley had arranged as a fun treat for the family.

"Do not ever make me get on a ship again," Anna warned her daughter after she silently sat through the boat ride.

Anna learned how to cook in the small Chicago apartment she shared with her parents and cousins, and later her own four children. Sometimes there was not enough sugar, or chocolate, or butter. But, nu, what do you do? The children needed to eat. So she'd make the food piping hot and stuffed with humorous surprises. The kids would delight in their attempts at stealing the carefully made pastries. They didn't notice that the filling was made from fried chicken skins that were the cheapest cuts at the butcher, or that they were often stuffed with more rice than meat. The kids would hold the golden pastries in their hands and see how their mother had rolled out the dough so carefully, it was thin enough to wrap the filling like it was a gift just for them.

My sister pulled the piroshkis out of the boiling oil. They were golden and fried and a bit more uniformed in size than when I had made them alone in Pittsburgh. We set our treats on one of my mother's large white dishes and arranged the platters on the dining room table. I took a picture of the food and texted it to Beverley.

Beverley messaged me back, "They look delicious."

Anna stood in the corner of the room with her full glass of cherry wine.

My mom reached for one of the hand pies and put it up to her lips.

Watching the Graves

My last relative in Alexandrovsky stood at the entrance of the town's Jewish cemetery. He wrapped his fingers around the locked metal gate and looked back at the tombstones sticking out of the earth.

"Who will watch the graves when I leave?" he asked himself.

His family was gone from this small village. Aunts, uncles, grandfathers, children—all settled in Chicago's West side. There they brewed cherry wine in apartment buildings taller than Alexandrovsky's highest church.

The family had been sending for him. They wrote him letters urging him to leave Russia before: Before the whispers of rumored violence turned into screams, before the border to the US closed to Jews for good. They promised him money for his ticket, a bed to sleep in when he arrived, and a job in the city.

But who would watch the graves when this last Jew was gone?

Every morning after he recited a personal shacharit he walked past the final row of houses into a wide field. A narrow path led through the tall grasses into the hilly pine forest that surrounded the shtetl. He knew this path well. He would step over roots, and past the quiet brook that ran wild in the spring. Up and up he would climb, all the while feeling the heavy weight of the cemetery key in his pocket.

At the top of the hill, the trees thinned out. There stood a rusted metal gate that enclosed the small Jewish cemetery.

Deftly, the man unlocked the gate and began his survey of the graves. First, he would walk down the center of the graveyard, noting which tombstones were chipping and would soon need repair. Next, traversing around the perimeter, he trimmed back overgrown grasses.

He would walk down each row of graves, forming a well-worn path through the village of the dead.

At the end of the morning walks he used to wait at the cemetery gate for the arrival of mourners. The cemetery was always busy with funerals, yartzheits, brides and grooms visiting the deceased before their wedding, and old women coming to garner blessings from the dead.

In the month of Elul, when Jews were instructed to visit the graves of their ancestors, the cemetery teemed with visitors from the moment the gates opened until he shut them before Ma'ariv. He would call in Yeshiva boys to help him manage the swarm of people. No matter what he tried, the crowds would rush through the cemetery, strewing pocketfuls of rocks onto tombstones and trampling over his well-cut paths.

He didn't mind the month's chaos though. All day long the air was filled with whispers and wails of, "Zichrona l'vracha," *May their memory be a blessing*, until it felt like the wind was praying alongside the Jewish people of Alexandrovsky.

But now he waited alone at the front gate. It was quiet. He could see a small blackbird flying in a circle overhead. The wind was still.

He looked behind him and closed the gate, locking it and carefully placing the heavy key in his pocket. He walked back down the path through the forest and the field, crossing the quiet row of houses at the edge of the shtetl.

Entering his home, he looked out his window. On the street, there was not a hum nor a stir. There was not a single bird flying outside.

"Where have you been?" he asked, waiting for a voice to answer him. But there was only silence on the old Jewish street.

He didn't want his descendants to remember him leaving. He wanted to stand like a guard at the gates of his peoples' graves, waiting until the bodies of his loved ones were revived in the streets of the emptying shtetl.

"Where have you been?" he'd shout as aunts, uncles, grandfathers, and children rushed back into the village with stories of far, far away worlds.

But the man was only human. He too was scared of the whispers that might turn into screams.

On his desk was the letter he would mail to his family, telling them to send over the ticket. He knew they would greet him at the dock, holding him with tears in their eyes.

"We can't believe you're alive!" they would shout.

And he would cry too. Each morning. As the aleynu of shacharit ended, he would remember the small path through the field. As kaddish began, he'd put his hand in his pocket, feeling for the heavy key to unlock the gate.

"Help me watch the graves?" he'd ask his children, and grandchildren, and finally me.

I don't know how to tell him that I can't find his shtetl on a map. I've never even been to the graveyard in Chicago where he is buried along with the other Rosenbergs. I don't have the key to the cemetery in my pocket.

I don't know who is watching the graves anymore.

What We Bury

It was Pesach in Indianapolis. My father's grandmother, Esther, was young with six children. She stood in her home's small backyard with a shovel in her hand, heaving her shoulder so the blade would pierce deeper and deeper into the barely thawed earth. Her breathing became slower. She bent down and lifted piles of crumbling dirt from the shallow hole she was digging.

Inside the apartment, my grandmother Rinky, just a little girl, screamed as her older brother tricked her out of the popcorn she'd bought for a dime. On the street corner, an organ grinder cranked out tinny Italian music while his small monkey held a cap out for money. Harsh smells of freshly grated horseradish and car grease wafted out of the apartment. Esther stood under the one tulip tree in the backyard, its buds just beginning to show. She wiped the mud from her hands onto her apron.

It was Pesach in Chicago. My mom's mom, Joyce, was running through the dining room, setting the long table for a big family meal. Her mother, Hazel, walked in front of her, elegant as always, folding napkins into small triangles. Joyce whispered, "F-O-R-K. L-E-F-T," to remember which side to put the silverware. She trailed her finger along the beautiful plates, tracing the small peaches and shimmers of silver adorning the dishes' edges.

In the kitchen, a large pot of chicken bones, carrots, and onions boiled on the stove. The room was dark; the one window illuminated the faded flowers on the grease stained wallpaper. Here Joyce's grandparents sat by the warm stove sewing piece work garments while they picked at the big platter of brisket and potatoes. They talked to one another in hushed Yiddish.

It was Pesach in Chicago. My mom's grandfather, David, held a sealed envelope in his hand, folding it between his fingers. He stood in the small front room which was filled with mismatched chairs and pushed together card tables. Shrieks of Yiddish gossip rose from the kitchen at the back of the apartment. His sister brought out dishes of salt water and parsley and placed them next to the bottles of cherry and grape wine.

"You gonna open that?" she quipped as she peered over David's shoulder.

"Not now, not now," he barked. "I'm tired from work, I've barely sat down and now I have to be the family's receptionist?"

"Alright then, have it your way," she breathed out heavily and returned to the laughter of the kitchen.

The letter was postmarked from Kiev, the biggest city next to the shtetl of Vasiklov where David's parents and one sister, Bat Sheva, still lived. His two sisters were twins, but only one had been able to make it to America so far.

The address on the envelope was written in shaky English letters that did not look like the handwriting of anyone he knew. He folded the envelope into thirds and put it in his pocket.

In Indianapolis, Esther knelt next to the shallow hole she had dug. She reached her hand into the cold ground so the dirt coated the grooved lines on her palms.

"I think it's deep enough," she murmured to herself, feeling the bottom of the hard, packed earth.

"Willy! Rinky!" she called back to the house. "Come bring the dishes!"

Esther could faintly hear little Rinky wailing.

"It's too heavy for me!"

"Come on, quit being a baby," her brother Willy chided.

The clanking of metal plates drowned out the children's bickering.

Esther turned around and watched the kids waddle towards her, their short arms full of dishes stacked high. Cups and cutlery perched at precarious angles atop the mountainous piles.

"Here," Willy huffed. He and Rinky dumped their dishes with a loud clatter onto the ground next to their mother. Rinky sighed with exaggerated exhaustion and draped herself over her mother's back.

"Up, up," Esther gently lifted her daughter off of her. She picked up the simple metal plates and inspected them in the early spring light.

In Joyce's Chicago dining room, she adjusted a vase of fresh cut purple and yellow flowers.

"Those look lovely," her mother cooed as she breathed in their scent.

"Thank you, Hazel," Joyce smiled up at her mother. The two were so close, Hazel let her young daughter call her by her first name.

"I think we're ready for dinner!" Hazel clapped her hands together, brimming at the perfectly set table.

"Mama! Papa! Kumt arayn," she called out. The old bobe and zeyde shuffled out of the kitchen. Joyce pulled a chair out for her grandmother and took hold of her boney arm, guiding her as she settled into her seat. Joyce sat on the opposite side of the long table, in the farthest chair from her grandmother. She watched the way the old woman's liver-spotted skin hung on her arms as she trembled, reaching for her glass of water. The little girl wondered what it would feel like to have a body that sagged and moved in such odd ways.

"Oh. Ikh hob fargesn epes," *I forgot something,* the zeyde announced.

"Forgot what now?" Hazel asked as she straightened a slightly askew fork.

Without answering his daughter, the old man shuffled back into the dark kitchen.

"Ay, Papa, yetst iz di tasyt far di sude," Hazel said, exasperated.

Joyce listened to the strange language of adults. She would learn it when she was their age, she thought.

In the kitchen, the zeyde was opening and shutting cupboard doors with increasing worry.

"Vu iz dos?"

"Where's what papa?"

"Di matse."

"Papa, I told you," Hazel walked into the kitchen and whispered. "Mir darfen nisht keyn matse." *We don't need matzoh.* "We have brisket and gefilte fish. And Joyce and I got rolls and cookies for dessert. We have enough food."

"Ober haynt iz Peysekh. Vos zogtsu?" *But today is Pesach. What are you saying?*

The old man continued to open and shut the cupboards, searching for the box of matzoh he'd bought from the little Hassidic boy who came selling it door to door.

"Papa! Genug." *Enough.*

"Aha!" He shouted in triumph, pulling the box of matzah from the cabinet above the sink. He held the cardboard above his head like a trophy.

"Mir hobn matse!" *We have matzoh!*

"Fine, fine. Just come sit down before the food gets cold," Hazel relented as she pulled a chair out for her father next to her mother. "Sit. Please."

David felt the letter in his pocket as he changed out of his work shirt. Bits of sawdust from the carpentry shop fell to the floor. He took out the pay from that week and fanned the bills in front of him. Biting on the inside of his cheek, he began to count out how much he would put aside for the ship tickets for his sister, Bat Sheva, and parents, still in Ukraine. The summer was coming which meant the kids would need shorts and maybe some new shoes. His wife, Anna was pregnant with their third child so expenses were about to shoot up—

"David! We're starting!" his sister called from the front room. He shoved the money in a box under his bed and finished changing into his button-down shirt. He could hear the rowdy family filling glasses with cherry wine. The smell of his sister's famous golden chicken soup floated into his room. He could hear her yelling at the boys to stop stealing matzah balls from the pot.

"Save some for dinner, you thieves!" she screamed joyfully.

He smiled, thinking of his two sisters, born at the same time and now separated by such a wide ocean. When they were girls, they looked so similar his mother had to put them in different colored dresses so people could tell them apart. He wondered if they'd still look so alike once they were together again.

"We're waiting for you, David!" His sister yelled at him. "You are not so important that you can keep your pregnant wife waiting for the Seder to start. God knows when we'll be able to eat at this rate. You're going to starve the woman!"

"Alright, alright, I'm coming," David shouted back. He felt around in the pocket of his work shirt and grabbed the folded envelope, ripping it open as he walked to the table.

Under the tulip tree in Indianapolis, Willy and Rinky handed Esther dishes from the big pile strewn on the frosty ground. Esther laid each one in the hole she had dug. The dishes made a stifled crash as they fell against one another; the cold earth muffling the vibrations.

Esther reached back her hand for another dish.

"Mama, that's the last one," Rinky said.

"Good. Let's fill the hole in now," Esther stood up and took the shovel back in her hands and began scooping the pile of dirt next to her with a quick, methodical motion. Avoiding their mother's darting blade, the children grabbed handfuls of dirt and threw them into the hole with pomp, watching how the pieces of Earth splayed out in the air like fireworks.

They slowly filled the hole until all of the dishes from the house were completely buried.

Esther breathed out in contentment and wiped the small sheen of sweat from her forehead with the back of her hand.

Willy leaned against his mother and looked up at the woman, her muscles swelling against her small frame.

"Mama, why are we burying the dishes before Pesach?"

Esther smiled and her cheeks blushed red with a sudden self consciousness of how strange she must appear to this little boy, living in an apartment in Indianapolis, so far from the village of Vishay where her mother taught her this practice.

"On Pesach, you must remove all of the bread from your house," she explained, "Even the smallest crumb on a plate. So most of the time, we have a new set of nice dishes we use for the holiday."

"Like those pretty ones they're selling at the department store?" Rinky asked.

"Yes, like that. But this year, we're not buying a second set of dishes. It's just too hard to spend money right now."

Willy nestled his head deeper into his mother's skirt, breathing in the cold spring air as it mixed with the comforting scent of roasted garlic emanating from her long dress.

"My mother taught me that, instead, you could bury your dishes in the backyard for 24 hours. And while the Earth is holding them, all of the little crumbs come off the plates. When we take them out they are kosher; ready for our Pesach feast."

"So they become like the dishes at the department store?" Rinky asked excitedly, imagining her worn metal plates transforming into the elegant shimmering dishes as they sat in this earthen pit.

Esther laughed, enjoying the fantasy of children on a chilly spring day.

Joyce poked her fork at the slices of brown meat on her plate, preferring the wine soaked raisins and apples in the fruit salad her grandparents kept calling "charoset."

"Isn't this lovely?" Hazel smiled at her husband and three children as she dished green bean casserole onto their plates. Joyce watched her beautiful mother. Her hair tied up in small buns on her head, a pearl necklace resting against her collarbone. She knew she had the prettiest mom of anyone in her class.

Her grandmother blew her nose into her lace napkin. The box of matzoh was opened next to her. She kept dipping her hand into the box, and breaking off small bits of the cracker to eat. Matzoh crumbs hung on the edge of her lips and fell in a small dusting on the front of her dress.

Next to Joyce was a basket of dinner rolls her mother had picked up from the bakery down the street.

"It's a holiday!" Hazel had explained earlier that day as she undid the twine ribbon on the box of pastries and breads. Joyce opened the box and stared with delight at the holiday treats.

The two had arranged the cookies on a platter for dessert while her grandparents and mom argued about something in Yiddish.

"We are American, Jewish just by name," her mother had explained in her kind but firm voice to her parents. She kissed them on the head and they looked up at her with the trusting eyes of a tourist being led by a local.

Joyce reached for one of the fluffy rolls on the Passover table and bit into it.

Her grandfather whispered some Hebrew words under his breath and ate his matzoh buried under a pile of charoset.

David walked into the sunny front room in Chicago. The mismatched chairs and pushed together tables were now filled with the scrubbed faces and coiffed hair of his wife's aunts and uncles and cousins. They nudged one another and caught up on the week's happenings as they squeezed in around the train of card tables. The little kids grabbed the hard boiled eggs stacked in bowls around the table while the adults poured eachother giant glasses of wine with mischievous eyes.

David's sister walked out of the kitchen, blowing on a spoon of her chicken broth. She looked up at her brother. He was standing in the doorway of the front room, not moving.

"What's the matter, David?" she yelled across the room over the chatter, trying to feign ease. David didn't answer her. His cheeks turned red and his eyes started to fill.

"David," she said tersely, jerking the spoon away from her lips. The golden broth spilled to the floor.

David held up the envelope. The chatter in the room hushed as people took notice of David and his sister.

His sister's lower lip began to tremble, but she balled her hands into fists as if fighting could stop the tears.

"You tell me what's in that letter!" she yelled. The room fell silent. David's wife let out a cry, holding her pregnant stomach. Everyone could guess what was in the letter. It was like torture for the young woman to make David say it out loud.

"Burial certificates." Tears streamed down David's cheeks. The children at the table stared in fear at the crying man. "For mama, papa, and Bat Sheva. They were killed in a pogrom."

David's sister grabbed her face with her hands, feeling her cheeks and nose and eyelashes, imagining her sister's face beneath her fingers. She stumbled back against the door frame and then sunk to the ground in a silent wail.

What do we bury when we come to Amerkie?

Esther dug up the dishes from the backyard. Rinky ran out, excited for her pretty new plates to come out of the earth—only to see the same drab metal she'd been eating off every other day of the year.

Joyce finished eating and sat at her end of the Passover table, listening to the grown-ups argue about this and that in Yiddish. She nibbled on the cookies decorated with Easter eggs.

David's wife had her baby months later. David held the little girl in his arms and felt her small cheeks, nose, and eyelashes under his fingertips. He named her Beverly after his sister, Bat Sheva, buried by strangers in a land that no longer knew his family's name.

This essay is dedicated to Pearl Roth, the last surviving of Esther and Michael Leventhal's six children. She lived to be 100 years old. She was buried in Indianapolis on the 11th of Tevet, 5783 (January 4th, 2023) while I was writing this essay.

To my people in the graveyard in Poland

5th of Av, 5781
Starachowice, Poland
From: Ami Lev Weintraub Ben Aviva v Yosef Aaron

To my people in the graveyard in Poland,

I imagine the trees growing tall around your buried bodies. Their wide leaves shade the long grasses that cradle rows of your tombstones. Maybe there's a big field with streams of sun that caress bursts of wild strawberries or a river rushing by with water from melting mountain snow.

Thank you trees and rivers for taking care of these bones.

I imagine my people, laid into this open earth, in a town that once knew your names. Your bodies are covered only in a white sheet. You rest so close to the dirt that roots from birch trees share their breath with you.

The Wailing Women cried at your funerals. Tears streamed over their quivering mouths as your families looked on in a stiff daze. The women's crackling songs opened doorways of grief that most people feared would swallow them whole. But these keening women crossed the perilous thresholds—for you.

I imagine the children leaving stones atop your graves. They turn the rocks in their hands and the jagged edges graze their soft skin. They pile the stones into high mountains only to watch them tumble down into the dust.

The town bustles with life at the news of your death. Rabbis rush to create a minyan, families cook platters of food. White candles burn on wooden mantles—their smoke carrying the town's prayers up to you.

You taught me how to hold the dead and the grieving in my own hands.

Thank you for caring for my bones.

I imagine you, my people, in the graveyard in Poland. Beautiful instead of destroyed. When the overgrown vines entangle your cracked gravestones, I try to imagine it is just the land holding you, remembering you, when there is no one left here who knows your name.

I am trying to imagine that all my people were buried with white sheets, wailing women, burning candles, children with rocks in their hands. In this daydream I gather the bones of the forgotten and murdered. My forgotten, my murdered. And I bury them next to you with white sheets, wailing women, burning candles, children with rocks in their hands.

I let this dream live in my mind so it may exist somewhere on this earth.

I am trying to bury our pain next to the bursts of strawberries growing in the streams of sunlight. To wash our hands in the rushing, snowy rivers. To let our mountains of grief tumble, and turn into dust.

Let us rest in these lands that know our names. Cradled by long grasses, shaded by wide leaves. The tall trees, growing higher each day.

Thank you for caring.

Let me know you have received this letter.

Zichrona Lee'vra'cha,

Ami Lev Weintraub Ben Aviva v Yoseph Aaron

Zingen un Tantsn

"When we are together again," the old Lithuanian man with the big eyes says at the end of our family Zoom call, "All I want is for us to zing and tants. Like we used to."

Zing un tants. Bereznitsky and Leventhal. The branches of the tree intertwining again.

"In Vilnius we had a dance troop," the old man from Lithuania tells my sibling and me after most people have left the family reunion Zoom call. I interlace my hands, feeling my physical body ground me as I dissolve into the uncanny feeling of long-lost people suddenly materializing on a screen.

The man tells us new stories of this distant land we were not supposed to speak of. My body relaxes as I hear the old country drawl in his voice. "We would gather to sing and dance the songs we'd learned in our village in Vishay."

In Vishay, he tells us, they had a huge, Jewish band. They marched around with slick black clarinets, golden tubas wrapped around their bodies, cymbals glowing and crashing like stars exploding into one another. The musicians would trail parades, weddings, brises, and funerals. They piped out cheerful and somber tunes as if in one united voice. Neighbors from far and wide would come to Vishay to listen to the marching band.

"And the cantors," he says. "We had beautiful cantors in shul."

My dad nods his head. He told me earlier about his grandfather, Michael. In his old age, he would sit in the corner of a room, chanting cantorial music to himself. The melancholy notes he'd learned in Vishay tumbled from his mouth for an audience of one. He sang in arm chairs, next to steaming ovens, in front of car washes, while children ran around, laughing with one another. He hardly noticed the moving world around him

After the Zoom call my new cousin sends me a video of his grandfather, my grandma Rinky's cousin. For an hour the old man walks around his Villnus apartment, singing songs from his childhood. The tunes abruptly move from mournful to upbeat to marching. Somber notes carry the grandpa's many syllables of Yiddish, Russian, Lithuanian, and Hebrew. I repeat the few words I know in each tongue.

In every song the grandfather stands up straight, shoulders back, his face blank save for a slight smile after the final breath. He croons unceremoniously throughout the house; he sings in a doorway, next to a gurgling sink, in front of an overflowing bookshelf, while three guests pour glasses of wine and laugh with one another.

He makes unbreaking eye contact with the camera. I feel like he is singing to me. I laugh but he doesn't react to my smiles. I want him to reach out from the tiny screen, take my hand, invite me into his apartment. I want him to sit me on the chair in his small library and teach me the songs he sang as a little boy. He is my grandmother's cousin. I want to sing with a man who should have known me.

On a cool summer night, two days before my 26th birthday, sheet music and Torah trope are spread across the table on the front porch where my dad and I sit. He is teaching me how to chant Torah.

"This is from the 80s, when I took a free class on Torah reading," my dad explains as he flips through the carefully saved pages of music.

He tells me how his grandfather Michael would go up to the Torah in his shul in Indianapolis and, without any preparation, chant the parsha with perfection.

"It's just what he learned how to do in Vishay," my father explains.

We sometimes find my dad sitting alone, humming music from the folk songs and jazz pieces he is working on. He spends nights preparing for the Torah chanting and lay-service leading he does at synagogue. Everyone says he is a beautiful cantor. They ask where he learned to sing like that and he shrugs his shoulders.

The crickets chirp their own tune as my dad points to the beginning lines of the Torah. He shows me the places where the notes go up like a jagged cliff, and then drop off suddenly. I try to copy his voice but the tune emerges harsh from my throat.

"It's all practice," he reassures me, as he listens to me slowly recite the first lines of the Torah again and again.

"And the land was tohhu v bohu (unformed chaos)," I sing in Hebrew. "And there was darkness on the face of the deepest depths of the sea."

I feel the words crash against the somber tune my father teaches me. And the land was unformed chaos. It is from this chaos that we all emerged. I imagine my great-grandfather singing these words over and over as a boy. It is in the darkness of the deepest sea that we all meet.

Later in the summer my sibling and I jump through our kitchen, twirling and waving our arms overhead. The warm summer light comes through the windows, splashes against the wooden floor and warms my back. My mother is embroidering on the sofa, my dad is practicing music in the basement. My sibling and I are learning Yiddish. We share our new-found words with one another like they are carefully wrapped gifts.

We shout, "Zing un tants!" As we dance through the kitchen in a frenzy of uncalled for, childish joy. I imagine the man with the big eyes swaying his body back and forth as his feet move in step with the dance troupe in Vilnius. I see his palms resting in the hands of the dancers to his right and left, deftly guiding their bodies through the spinning line dances he learned as a child. He dances with us. I can almost hear my great-grandfather and his nephew sing songs in a language my sibling and I will soon come to know.

The past and the present are learning a common tune, a shared dance.

In this moment we are safe—
To sing and dance,
just like we all used to.

I still speak

Here, Now

When I was in college, I wrote a fictional story about two Jewish girls in Eastern Europe. One night they wandered through the shadows of trees and climbed up and up a rocky incline. In the darkness of the hilltop they confessed their secret love to each other.

Weeks later, as the girls held hands on this moonlit hill, they saw men on horseback gallop into their town with lanterns and axes.

"Cossacks," they whispered in terror.

The men lit the sleeping fictional town on fire. Tucked away on the hilltop, the girls watched the wooden synagogue burn and heard their families scream. But their love for each other saved them; its secret hid them atop this shadowy hill while their world turned to ashes.

I wrote this story for a girl I loved but never told. I wrote, imagining that her embrace might save me from horror.

I read the piece to my fiction class at the University of Pittsburgh. The students were mostly white and from some mishmash of Christian upbringings across Pennsylvania. Every day I came into the class quietly, hardly speaking.

After I read my story, a girl with dirty blonde hair and a sippy-cup water bottle raised her hand to comment.

"I like the story but it doesn't seem factual," she said. "Things weren't that bad for Jewish people."

Other students jumped in to discuss the historical accuracy of my story. The teacher told me to write down "fact check" as a note for further revision.

I dreamt of the saving embrace of the fictional girl on the hill.

The biggest class I took at Pitt was Bible as Literature. The course met in a giant, stadium-like auditorium. The teacher stood in front of the massive audience and assured us he would teach the Bible from a purely literary and anthropological perspective.

I knew one boy in this giant room of people. I had met him at Hillel the two times I went. In class, he waved at me and I waved back. Sometimes I sat next to him when I felt lonely. Other times, I thought I was too cool for him; this Jewish boy who wore ill fitting polos and metal rimmed glasses. I would rather sit by myself with my hood pulled tight over my head.

The professor began the semester by teaching what he called the Old Testament. The book could be read as a metaphor for Jesus's coming, he said. It showed that the G-d of the Old Testament was wrathful and jealous unlike the kind and forgiving G-d of the New Testament.

I had never heard the Torah described this way. As a child, I would watch my parents and their friends lift the scroll out of the ark, cradle it in their arms and parade it around the congregation for everyone to kiss. It was like a newborn baby, hallowed and miraculous, a gift to the whole community.

When I studied Torah, my Rabbis and teachers asked me to explore the lines of the text over and over for layers of hidden secrets. They taught us that the G-d of the Torah was inexplicably uncategorizable. The friend, the redeemer, the hurt, the fierce, the rock, the breath, the wind. Sometimes wrathful and jealous but never just that.

In front of the eager audience of students, this man finally taught me the purpose of this book that my community kisses every Saturday morning. He assured us that he was a professor, teaching from an objective place.

I came into class one day and sat three rows away from the boy I knew. He waved at me and I feigned an interested smile.

The professor began class and I took out my notebook. He was teaching about the Mosaic laws and the Jews who still followed them. Because of their adherence to earthly mitzvot, he described Jews as materialistic, unspiritual; an archetype for Western standards for "primitive."

"What do the Mosaic laws tell us about the Jewish people?" he asked.

I looked back at my notes and raised my hand.

He called on me. The boy from Hillel caught my eye with a hopeful smile.

"It shows that the Jews are materialistic," I said. The boy's face dropped and his eyes glassed over. He looked away.

I had betrayed us both, and the Rabbis, the teachers, the friends who danced with the Torah and taught me its secretes. I had abandoned them for the approval of this man who said he teaches the objective truth. In front of this class of hundreds, I let these students nod their heads and affirm that Jews were just as greedy and materialistic as they thought.

I dreamed of apologizing to the boy.

I graduated a few years later with a degree in Jewish Studies. In my capstone paper, I wrote about Russian Public schools in the 1850s and how the government had explicitly created these schools to assimilate Jewish children into Russian culture. At the schools, they would teach their students a sanitized version of Judaism that was seen as less antagonistic towards Christian culture.

Jewish families resisted the schools with protests and boycotts that culminated in a standoff against Russian tanks in town squares on Passover. The Jews fought to continue teaching their children in their communities' traditional cheders and Yeshivas.

The school's Religious Studies Department hosted a joint graduation for their 50 graduates and the two of us graduating from the small Jewish Studies department. We all gathered in a small art gallery on campus. Somber Renaissance paintings encircled a sunlit courtyard filled with flowers about to bloom. One by one, the faculty called us up to the wooden podium at the front of the audience. They asked us to speak about our final research projects and what we planned to do next.

"I wrote about the way public schools in Russia assimilated Jews," I said into the microphone haltingly. "And I'm going to study Yiddish this summer. And after that, I'm not sure."

Everyone clapped. The professors handed me my degree and I sat back in my chair. I looked out at the budding flowers and listened as the students shared their studies and the careers they were choosing. There was only one other Jewish studies student. Nearly everyone else was Christian.

At the end of the ceremony, a teacher I didn't know pressed her hands together and grinned.

"Time for the photo!" she exclaimed. "In front of the painting."

The Religious Studies Department students laughed and hugged one another as they walked assuredly to the back of the art gallery. Everyone knew where to go so I silently followed these cheery people. They smiled and leaned down into a squat. I awkwardly bent down to match their practiced pose. Parents pulled out phones ready to take pictures.

"Oh my god," my mom exclaimed. She pointed behind me, her other hand covering her mouth.

I looked over my shoulder at the artwork we were gathered in front of.

It was a massive painting of Jesus, bloodied and nailed to a cross.

"Are you serious?" I said out loud.

My parents looked up at me and laughed nervously as horror crept onto our faces. In the photos they took of my Jewish studies graduation, I stare at them with bewildered shock in front of a painting of Jesus.

I dreamed of the Jewish families standing up against the tanks.

The Mundane and the Holy

Content Warning: this essay discusses the mass shooting at the Tree of Life synagogue.

No one talks about the mundane parts of tragedy.
Like the boxes we had to pack and move from the synagogue after the shooting.

The principal of the Dor Hadash Religious School gathered the teachers into the staff room at the shul down the street. It was our first day back at school since everything changed.

"We need to get the Hebrew books from the old building so we can keep teaching the kids," he said.

I slowly sipped water from a paper cup, feeling the wetness fill my dry mouth. Outside the sky was black, and a faint yellow glow emenated from the quiet city. The leaves were falling from the trees; plastic skeletons and fake graves dotted front lawns.

I opened my calendar on my phone to see if I had time to gather Hebrew books from a crime scene.

The next week, I carried five old boxes up the stairs to our new classrooms at the big synagogue down the street. Another teacher had gone into the Tree of Life building, packed the boxes, and loaded them into her car. The rest of the teachers and I couldn't bring ourselves to go back to the "old building" as we now called it.

Before school that day, we opened the beaten-up cardboard flaps in our new classrooms. We pulled out Hebrew primers, tiny red scissors, a bag of pompoms, aleph bet bingo boards, a blue plushie Torah.

"This is most of what I could find in there," explained the teacher who had gone back. I pushed aside a container of broken crayons so I could unroll the Hebrew Yoga poster that had hung on the wall in our kindergarten classroom.

She told us what she saw when she was filling the boxes and I tried not to listen.

"The windows were boarded up."

I focused on sorting the googly eyes by color and then size and then color again.

"There were these stains on the carpet," she continued.

I dragged a pair of tiny red scissors along the tape on a cardboard box addressed to the school. Every day we were sent a new package of "consolation gifts" from a church or middle school art teacher. We'd already gotten a stack of wooden stars decorated with uplifting messages and tubes of rolled up canvases painted with pictures of sunsets.

That day I unpacked the newest arrival: 30 "diverse" hand knit dolls that church ladies three states away made for us. I squeezed each plush body trying to understand what type of comfort people thought we needed. Secretly, I wished these gifts would be enough to make everything better.

I arranged the dolls on the table next to the books about Rosh Hashanah and the tall stack of white boards still covered in the shaky handwriting of children. "Nun's" blended into "Bets" as my students spelled out their AlephBet for the first time.

We unpacked everything we needed to keep teaching the children.

There is so much more I could say, but I don't want to scare you.

I don't want you to know the way After can reverberate for years. How a shattering of windows keeps vibrating through my bones no matter how far I am from Pittsburgh.

And I know you might have your own After. It trembles in its own way, pulsing through your muscles when you stretch just so, when that song comes on, when you go to sleep and try not to think about it anymore.

I want you to teach me how it moves in you.

I'm sorry they hurt your body too.

Once the news cameras left, once the next tragedy happened, once you stopped watching,
    we had to keep teaching the children
    to not fear their Jewish bodies.

Your grief for what you've lost
lifts a mirror up to where you're bravely working.

—Rumi

I want to talk about cardboard boxes. The mundane aspects of tragedy.

How after the funeral at the JCC we left out the side door because there were so many people. Someone had covered the muddy ground with flattened, cardboard boxes labeled "Emergency Gauze" so we wouldn't sink into the wet earth.

And the food we bought for the makeshift shiva came in huge, bulk Costco boxes. They took so long to load and unload into our friends' small cars. For days after, our arms ached from all of the lifting.

And how that Chanukah my co-teacher made a giant dreidel out of a cardboard box. It was big enough for the small six-year-old children to wear on their bodies. Adorned in the letters for "Nes, Gadol Haya, Sham, A great miracle happened there," they spun and spun and spun until they fell over from their dizziness.

Expecting the worst, you look,
and instead, here's the joyful face
you've been wanting to see.

—Rumi

On Purim that year the Tree of Life congregation performed a Purim spiel for the rest of the community.

"Don't kill the Jews!" they sang out to "Yellow Submarine" while dressed in Beatles costumes. I held back a mixture of tears and laughter. The words' hilarious poignancy made me hear them as if for the first time.

When the spiel was over I held hands with my first grade student. She was dressed as a cat, of course, and we wandered into the Purim carnival with its rows of brightly lit games. It was a typical Purim carnival. In the center of the room was a giant blow-up bouncy house which kids climbed up and tumbled out of in chaotic succession.

My student turned to look at me. She licked a rainbow snow cone. The ice rubbed against her painted cat whiskers, causing dark lines to run down her cheek.

"I don't tell people who I don't know that I'm Jewish," the six year old told me suddenly. A seventh grader ran by with reams of blue tickets curled in his hand.

"Ok," I said, panic building in my body. "Can you tell me more?" I asked. I was practicing the active listening skills a psychologist taught us in a thirty minute presentation.

"I don't want anyone to hurt me."

Your grief for what you've lost
lifts a mirror up to where you're bravely working.

—Rumi

Everything around me became a mirror.

Our city was grieving, but it felt like no one knew how to do it.

The Lyft driver picked me up from the house we all went to after we heard the news.

"It's a shame that happened," she said. "The Jews are good people. They just keep to themselves and don't make a problem."

The woman at the Children's Museum where I was working saw me wearing a kippah.

"Can I just give you a hug?" she said.

"Ok."

And we embraced quietly by the big metal sink where I was washing paint covered brushes. She cried while I held her.

Or the man at the bus stop who apologized to me when he learned I was Jewish.

"It's been hard," I said, trying not to scare him.

Three years later I gathered with two sets of sisters from my Hebrew school class. It was the fall of 2021, in the heart of the pandemic, and I was now their Hebrew school teacher and their Covid mini-school teacher. Every weekday morning I helped them with online classes while their schools were closed indefinitely.

At 9:00 a.m. sharp they logged in to their online class. They'd adjust their cheetah print cat-ear headphones and listen as their Zoom teacher clicked through a powerpoint while describing the schedule for the day. While their teachers talked, the girls played with the clay I bought them and sank into the bean bag chairs I brought from my childhood bedroom. When they finished their work, I gathered them together for our morning meeting. Here we decided what games we would play and what songs we would sing.

I pointed to the oldest girl in the class.

"Can you lead us in our closing song?"

She nodded and gestured for the other kids to stand. "We go on our tiptoes and move our arms like we are angels!" She explained, demonstrating the motions I was taught as a child in Hebrew school and had watched my parents do in services.

"Kadosh, Kadosh, Kadosh," the kids sang as they jumped on their tiptoes, "Holy, Holy, Holy."

Tiny masks covered the bottoms of their faces. They jumped around the room singing, "Kadosh, Kadosh, Kadosh." They danced while holding shimmering blue, yellow, and green scarves. The fabric followed their bodies so their movements froze behind them, just for a moment.

We didn't have to sing and dance. Their parents only asked me to help them with their online work and make sure they didn't flunk out of elementary school. But the way their scarves trailed their motions with color made us smile. Singing felt so good as the words vibrated in our throats. We took joy in reminding each other we were holy even while we social distanced from one another and wore masks to cover our mouths. The mundane aspects of tragedy.

After they finished singing their final song I sat with the children in a circle for our morning meeting. They laughed while we made up silly names for the dying spider plant we found in our building and had decided to take in as our own.

At the end of the meeting I cleared my throat nervously. The leaves were falling from the trees and the kids were discussing their intricate Halloween costumes. It was the season to talk about what had happened. Discussing tragedy was part of my job now.

"Do you know what day it is tomorrow?" I asked.

"It's the two year anniversary for something bad that happened at our synagogue," the sweet seven-year-old answered confidently. She was in my class when the shooting took place and I'd been teaching her at Hebrew school ever since.

"What happened two years ago?" the other second grade girls asked. They adjusted their masks on their faces and waited patiently for my answer, their big eyes staring intently at me.

I rubbed my palms on my pants and felt the shattering windows vibrate through my bones. The girls weren't at our Hebrew school the year of the shooting. Their parents never told them about the man who tried to kill us.

These are the parts of tragedy that are both so painful and so mundane now; who teaches the children about the hurt we carry?

I explained what happened. Their eyes widened behind their masks. I wanted to run away, hand them knit dolls from Church ladies, pack all of the confusion and hurt of the last two years into cardboard boxes we could bring back to the "old building."

"We don't want this anymore," I imagined saying, leaving our boxes of wounded parts at the foot of the Tree of Life.

Instead, I let them ask questions.

"Yes he had a gun, yes people were shot. Eleven people."

These details were still terrifying to me. But they had somehow become routine.

"But why did he do it?"

I paused. The question deviated from the script I'd made for myself. And the terror behind their question reminded me of the depth of my own fear.

Slowly I explained, "There's a long history of people who don't like Jews." The words felt like shards of glass in my mouth. They were seven and eight years old. They didn't know this story yet. How do I teach these sweet sisters about the people who hate them?

"But we are safe now. For now," I corrected myself. We were days away from the 2021 election, living in a city surrounded by Trump signs and Confederate flags. Many mornings I was scared someone would burst into our unlocked classroom while the children were playing.

Please don't be scared of yourself, I wanted to say to the children. You are so holy.

The kids nodded their heads and stood up clumsily, in a daze, pulling one another up from the floor. They picked up glittering hula hoops and spun them, fast and hard, on their outstretched arms. They moved with a frantic hyperness I had not seen before. The cascades of colorful scarves jumped with their scared motions. They stacked cardboard boxes and knocked them over, watching their towers tumble to the ground.

"Kadosh, Kadosh, Kadosh," they sang. "Holy, Holy, Holy."

Settle your bodies, I whispered to them.

Your hand opens and closes and opens and closes.
If it were always a fist or always stretched open,
you would be unable to move.

—Rumi

For now, we are safe.
For now, they sing and dance.

Birds with Fire

Never say this is the final road for you,
Though leadened skies may cover over days of blue.
As the hour that we longed for is so near,
Our step beats out the message—we are here!

—Zog Nit Kayn Mol
Song of the Partisans

It was January 2020, one of those winter days in Pittsburgh where the clouds hung so thick in the sky they turned the city's yellow bridges pale shades of gray. A flock of crows flew behind me, their bodies appeared like a looming shadow in my wake. Trump was on the verge of going to war with Iran and across the country people were gathering to protest.

I walked up to the street corner across from the Pitt library humming a song I can no longer remember. I joined the small group of people with fleece jackets, white hair, and nicely printed song sheets who were protesting the war. A tall, old white man held a microphone and led chants. I nodded to the people in black hoodies standing at the edge of the group.

"Get out!" someone yelled across the street.

I turned to look. It was my hot-headed friend. He was always the one starting something with someone at protests like this. Today he was screaming at a small group of men on the other side of the intersection. They were dressed in pastel polo shirts, holding signs that were hard to read from a distance. My friend snatched their posters and tore them in half.

"What's he up to again?" I laughed lightly, nudging a friend in a beaten-up leather jacket.

"He's yelling at Nazis," they said under their breath. "We kicked a bunch of them out a few minutes ago. They were holding signs that said rich Jews were pulling the strings for the war."

The murder of crows flew overhead and screamed in a curdling cacophony. I wished I could yell so shrilly.

"We can't let them be here!" the hot-headed friend shouted, gesturing for us to join him in protesting the Nazis.

The tall, old white man leading the demonstration interjected. "Let's sing," he said into the microphone.

The crowd cheered and threw their fists into the gray cloud-filled sky.

While they sang, a friend in a black denim vest raised their hand and pointed quietly at a man in a blue polo standing amid the group of singing people.

"There's still a Nazi over on this side of the street," they said. It was Greg Conte, a major instigator of the white nationalist "Unite the Right" rally in Charlottesville. "The organizers said he can stay if he doesn't cause a problem." They flicked the end of their cigarette and rolled their eyes. Even allowing a quiet Nazi to join the protest was allowing a Nazi to join the protest.

The throng of black crows overhead finally got tired of flying and descended en masse on a stand selling Belgian waffles. They preened their feathers while one hopped from her perch onto the brick-layed plaza. She stretched her large wing out, only to pull it back abruptly against her chest. She flapped, trying to take flight as she had done so many times before, but instead her wing hung at a skewed angle and she recoiled at the pain. As she settled into her flightless state, the crow turned her head towards the humans, her black eyes watched us sing.

"Anyone want to come up? Share their thoughts on the war?" the tall, old white man held the microphone out towards the crowd of people. A woman with silver hair and a sparkling scarf approached in a slow, halting walk.

"Thank you," she took the mic, cleared her throat and began to sing, "This little light of mine."

The crowd joined in.

I couldn't take my eyes off the Nazi.

"I'm gonna let it shine!"

My friend with the leather jacket tapped me on the shoulder. "If you go up there and say something about Conte we'll back you up, make sure he gets out of here."

I tried to refuse. "That seems like a lot."

But they insisted.

Where does the courage come from to confront what terrifies us? I looked up, but no angles of strength or messengers of bravery could penetrate the cloudy, leaden sky.

I remembered being in Poland with my youth group the winter I was 18. It was February and the sky was just as white and full of clouds as it was in Pittsburgh. They toured us around Warsaw, showing us potholes and apartment buildings, bus stations and cafes; each mundane place was a former site of Jewish resistance.

"At this park, a Jewish woman threw a Molotov cocktail at a Nazi government building," the guide pointed to an office building. We followed his finger and saw a group of children kicking a soccer ball back and forth, shouting as they defended a goal made from propped up soda bottles. A bird spiraled high above, watching us as we tried to imagine flames consuming the quiet playground.

The crowd clapped politely as the woman with the sparkling scarf finished singing.

"Who's next with something to share?"

I walked towards the center of the crowd and raised my hand. I could feel my heart beat deep in my chest.

The woman passed me the microphone. It felt like a heavy stone in my hand.

"Hello," I flinched at the booming sound of my voice. My friends waited for my cue. I would point to the Nazi. If he tried to talk back, they would kick him out.

The crow with the broken wing sounded a piercing shriek. I looked towards her cry and startled. A striking woman I hadn't seen earlier stood next to the bird. She wore a long black dress that cascaded like a puddle at her feet. Her brown hair was streaked red and orange and flowed down her back in a loose braid. She held a glass bottle in her hands with a white cloth hanging from its mouth. She seemed to flicker in and out of focus as the wind blew.

"Go on," I heard her say, but her lips never moved.

I focused back on the microphone in my hand, the crowd of people dressed in fleece, the man in the blue polo.

I pointed firmly at Greg Conte.

"Why have we let a Nazi be at this protest?"

His eyes lit up with surprise as my fingertip found his face. He took a shocked step backwards. *You got me*, his open, unspeaking mouth seemed to say.

All I wanted was for him to denounce that he was a Nazi, say it was all a mistake.

I wanted this battle between me and the Nazis to be a game. One the grownups were taking too seriously. Like when a kid got upset after losing at kickball and started calling the other team names. We would all tell him to get over it and laugh at him for believing that this game, with its made-up, human rules had any importance, that its outcome was significant enough to cause anger.

As a child I remember watching the sunlight fall gently between the oval leaves of trees. I was falling in love with the world for the first time. I was discovering that when the sun flowed through trees, it created opalescent, green shadows. This fact of nature seemed like the only rule that meant anything at all.

Here's your chance to stop this, Greg Conte.

But instead he smiled.

"Will you let me talk?" he said.

"Nazis out! Nazis out!" my friend in the leather jacket chanted on cue.

"You had better listen to the truth. We could have a discussion. Are you that afraid of what I have to say?" Conte yelled.

The crowd surrounded him.

"What's happening?" The tall, old white man who organized the anti-war protest rushed over and waved his arms in alarm. The mass of perched crows took off and flew above his head, leaving behind the one with the broken wing.

I watched as the crowd rose and fell with a cohesive unity. Like a wave moving a piece of driftwood to shore, they slowly walked Conte towards the edge of the sidewalk, making him leave with a gentle force.

The woman in black smiled at me with piercing eyes. The remaining crow nestled her head into the folds of the black skirt. The woman bent down and held the bird's broken wing in her hand.

I chanted "Nazis out!" into the microphone as a thin shadow fell across my shoulders. The tall, old white man was standing above me, with one hand on his hip, the other pointed at my face.

"What do you think you're doing?" Spit glistened on the side of his lip.

"There shouldn't be Nazis here," I said calmly.

"You've made this quiet gathering into a riot," he stammered.

"It's not a riot." Angry heat splashed across my cheeks.

The woman in black reached into her pocket and pulled out a small, wooden match. She rubbed it between her fingers. In her other hand she held the glass bottle with the white rag hanging from its mouth. The bird hopped onto her shoulder, its wing unfurled a bit straighter.

"But there's Nazis here! Why not have a riot?" I retorted.

"Because this chaos is all the papers are going to report on." His hand wildly cut through the air like the motor on a boat. He pointed at the wave of people gently moving Conte away. "The reporters are going to ignore how peaceful we had been before this."

The woman struck a match against her shoe. Her hair came loose from its braid. Its red and orange strands splayed around her like a roaring inferno. She held the flame up to the glass bottle. Its glow illuminated the black pellets packed tight into the vessel's belly.

Peaceful?

We were at war, me and this Nazi. We've been at war for generations. There has not been peace between us for so long. But the singing people at the protest were not part of this battle. They didn't hear the ghosts who wailed in my ears. They did not feel this war in the twists of their stomachs. They could still stand next to a Nazi and be at peace.

Where did their courage come from?

"Get out of my face," I yelled.

The woman in black buried the flame into the bottle's white rag. A dancing spark sprinted into the belly of the vessel.

The tall, old white man looked at me with shock at what I had said to him.

"Do you not have any respect for your elders?"

The woman smashed the molotov cocktail to the ground.
The flames consumed me.

In Poland the Jewish guides reiterated the lesson our Torah school teachers taught us as kids, that our suffering made us responsible to stand against the suffering of others; that we must fight back when we feared we might be hurt. I wondered what this tall, old white man learned as a child; perhaps he learned songs with tunes as peaceful as a dove's cry. Perhaps his parents never taught him about the women who throw molotov cocktails to survive.

"Nazis out!" the crowd continued to chant.

The crow screamed, flapped its wings and flew off into the thick, leaden sky.

> *Never say this is the final road for you,*
> *Though leadened skies may cover over days of blue.*
> *As the hour that we longed for is so near,*
> *Our step beats out the message—we are here!*
>
> *The early morning sun will brighten our day,*
> *And yesterday with our foe will fade away*
> *But if the sun delays and in the East remains—*
> *This song is a password, generations must maintain.*
>
> *This song was written with our blood and not with lead,*
> *It's not a little tune that birds sing overhead.*
> *This song a people sang amid collapsing walls,*
> *With grenades in hand they heeded to the call.*

—Zog nit keynmol
Song of the Partisans

Why do you stay?

At night, I dangled my feet off the Edge of the World and watched the hills across the valley shimmer with stars. Elias pointed at the pink and purple sky framed by the Bloomfield bridge.

"The most beautiful sunset in the world," they whispered as they held my hand for the first time.

In Pittsburgh the seasons pass with laughter as we witness the city's imperfect beauty.

In the spring a family of groundhogs wriggle out of their hiding place in the valley I cross on my way to work. They burrow in the overgrown bushes that peek out between the Hyundai dealership and the train tracks. Cars rush by as I stand on the overpass sidewalk. One after another the goofy creatures stand on their furry hind legs as we watch each other on the bridge they call home.

"I swear there's 10 of them over there," I told Cat.

"You'll have to take me to see it. That's too magical for me to believe," she laughed.

In the summer the gray concrete turns into a jungle of knotweed. Each forgotten patch of earth blooms with the towering green stalks.

At an overgrowth by her house Corrine yanked the giant shoots out with all of her might. "It leaches lead from the soil, so it grows really well here," she laughed at the plants who found home in such poisoned earth.

A few months after the knotweed crops up, the morning glories arrive. They wrap around every street sign and fence.

"They're eating our table!" Lexi announced one morning, pointing to the vines of deep purple and bright pink flowers climbing up the legs of our patio furniture.

Our deck chairs are covered in soft petals, like a throne of watercolor flowers arriving to anoint us. If we sit out there too long, we joke, the vines might curl around our arms and legs and pin us in place. To be captured by flowers, I smile at the thought.

In the fall the birds leave again. I stood outside with Barukh and for what felt like an hour we watched flock after flock of little black birds fly overhead. Their dark silhouettes looked like a careful etching against the pink evening sky.

"I feel like they are carrying us away with them," Barukh said.

Then winter comes and destroys everything. For months the sun doesn't emerge from behind the thick white clouds. The streets buckle under the cold and cracks erupt into sinkholes so big they swallow buses. Water mains burst and cover the steep hills with thick layers of ice. One winter, Tahel, Flip and I slipped backward and were forced to crawl up these icy hillsides. We laughed in sheer terror at the power of the world.

For three years I woke up each morning in Elias's bed and they taught me how to make it through these cold months. In the car they played me music they sang with their friends in high school.

"This winter hasn't been so rough / It was cold but it wasn't cold enough / To freeze the blood beneath my spine / At least I survived."[1]

When the Spring comes, the city buzzes with the adrenaline-fueled thrill that we made it.

And the groundhogs peek out of their hiding spots with new babies. They wriggle and stand on hind legs and greet me as I walk to work.

This is the rhythm of the changing earth in Pittsburgh.

Why do you stay?

My mom asks.

Because of the groundhogs, and the morning glories, and the way the hills glisten with stars; because the seasons make us laugh and fall in love and remember the people who are now gone.

This land has cradled me in its valleys for seven years now. I've walked her bridges in protest, in terror, in love. Her rivers are a

---

1 *Dark Days* by Pup

promise I make to myself. I will look at the waters each time I cross these faded yellow bridges. Look! Even on the way to work, tired and cold at 7:30 in the morning.

When I first moved to the city I had no friends and I decided, one day, to ride from Oakland to the Northside. I got on the 54c bus and we wound our way up through Polish Hill and rose into the fog-covered neighborhood. Each turn up the narrow, one-way road revealed a new secret; a cluster of tall trees with deep green leaves, a sudden expanse of blue sky, a glistening river rushing into Downtown. I wanted to cry at the beauty. I was so lonely. But the hills wanted to know me.

Why do you stay?

My hands clutch this land even though Elias and Izzy moved away. Tahel left for six months. Matteo and June have been in and out of the city for years now. I still hold on tight to this earth.

But it's not mine. I know that.

I'm not from here. This place has caused me a pain that will never allow me to feel fully at ease here.

And this land belongs to another people. It is the traditional lands of the Adena culture, Hopewell culture, and Monongahela peoples. Refugees of other tribes including the Delaware, Shawnee, and Haudenosaunee also made a home by these three rivers. British, French, and American colonizers took this land with genocidal force from the Indigenous peoples here. And I live here because of their violence.

So why do you stay?
On these lands that are not yours?
On these lands where you will never fully be accepted?

Because the End of the World is just a parking lot at the edge of a hillside. And a jungle of knotweed means the soil is going to poison us all one day. And the stars in the hills are just porch lights shimmering on distant, winding roads.

"The nature here is so honest," Lexi says one night.

The city is made up of imperfect beauty.

I see myself clearly in these murky waters.

One night, Lexi, Leo, and I walked along the gravel road that meanders next to the river. A canopy of brambles and trees obscured the flood lights from the warehouse nearby.

We could just barely hear the lapping of the water. We watched the nearly full moon shine over the candles we arranged in a circle. I was getting top surgery in a few days, on the full moon of Tishrei. We gathered to let the waters help me let go and change. No one swims in this river anymore, but we still come to these shores to find something holy.

In a land etched with the scars of industry, the sacred emerges in mysterious ways. A few weeks after Corrine died, I rummaged through a "Take something, leave something" box nailed to a stump at the End of the World. I pulled out a zine titled, *All About Knotweed*. The leaded soil and the plants who are nourished by it helped a friend say hello.

A year later, a flock of black birds landed in a pack when we held a Tree of Life commemoration ceremony in the parking lot at Hebrew school.

"Why are there so many birds here?" nine-year-old Opal asked as the air filled with the cacophony of their squawks.

"They're migrating," I tried to explain with a teacher's confidence.

She raised her eyebrows at me, not accepting my answer. "That can't be the only reason they are here."

Her assurance invited me to return to the earth's magic. She hadn't yet learned to doubt it.

It's been seven years.
I've been held by these hills
and hurt so deeply.
At the park near Ritters I lean against the white bark of the American Sycamore. She teaches me how to become her friend and I love her for this lesson.

But as I rest against her I remember the birch trees in Vishay. I hear the forest of thin branches calling me back to my ancestor's lands.

It's been 100 years
since my family has been held by those white trunks
and hurt so deeply.
I imagine the lake cut in two in the village where my great-grandmother's family were fishermen. They lived right along the water. They could hear the tree frogs croaking and smell the sweet scent of purple orchids. They watched the lake freeze in winter and thaw out again

in spring. In summer, barely dressed children dove into the sloshing waters and crouched and ate blueberries in the shade of the trees.

How did they let go of this land so many jubilees passed?

The earth tells our story of imperfect beauty.

Narrow alleys lined with faded pastel houses frame the most beautiful sunset in the world. The vista is an overlook from a parking lot.

But can it last longer? I ask Elias in vain, wanting to stop the last bit of color from fading into the royal blue of the night sky. It's getting warmer again. Elias is moving to Berlin in June. The stars are coming out on this moonless night. The cicadas begin to chirp from their hiding place within the newly sprouting knotweed.

I hold on tight to how things are, but the trees are growing buds on their naked winter branches. As always, the hills remind me that change is coming.

In this seventh year, I ask the land one last favor.

Teach me how to let go.

Coiled Potential

Pittsburgh, Summer 2020

There was a quiet dance. When the Nazi pulled the gun and pointed it at the people dressed in black denim and silver studs. It was behind the dive bar on Liberty Avenue at two in the afternoon. Cars drove by like usual, not seeing the people stumbling forward and backwards in a petrified rhythm. The people-turned-dancers waved their arms above their heads and took two steps back—elegantly fearful. They waited for the next beat. That piercing crack, coiled in the potential of finger on trigger.

Across the street I knelt behind a parked car. My muscles braced. I beheld the terrifying silence of two possible futures struggling to be born.

In an instant, the man finished the dance.

Decisively, he ran back to his car.

The gun unchanged.

No blasts. No sparks.

The final beat, still just a potential.

He revved his engine, pulled out, and flew down the street. The synchronized dance broke apart.

The people scattered in all directions.

And I knelt behind the parked cars, unchanged.

No blasts. No sparks.

Only the potential of finger on trigger now coiled in my body.

In the weeks after it happened I tried to hide this Nazi from my family. It became my secret. Like I had been the one holding the gun. Like my parents were my seven-year-old Hebrew school students who pronounced the word "Nayy-zeee" because they had never heard it said before.

How do you tell a child what has happened to us?

"We are all adults," my mom tells me when she hears the clicking of the gun inside my twisted stomach.

I just didn't think I would tell her about this again.

Nazis in my neighborhood for the fifth time in two years.

They shook hands with the police officers called to the scene.

Of course.

The cops let them walk away.

Of course.

Nazis. The cops let them walk away.

I'm waking up from a long dream.

It's summer in Pittsburgh. I'm walking down Liberty, sweat sticking my black tank top to my stomach. I'm listening to my dad sing folk songs through my noise-canceling headphones.

"They're trying to wash us away."

Friends text me about the Nazis passing out fliers two blocks from my house. A woman in a neon yellow helmet swooshes by on a silver bicycle.

"They're trying to wash us away." I listen to the lullabye my dad sang me to sleep with when I was a child.

I'm in front of the brick hospital with the green awnings, across from the anarchist bookstore that is also our home. A number 54 bus inches past and wheezes with the exhaustion we all feel on this summer day in Pittsburgh. I watch the Nazis pin fliers on shop doors and wave signs scrawled with red writing.

Ten minutes later the cops will shake their hands.

Five minutes after that, the Nazi will point a gun in my friend's face.

"They're trying to wash us away," the final reprise of the chorus fades out.

I went to see the Nazis because I wanted to behold what I feared in all of its detail.

If I didn't go, I worried, someone might brush it off saying,
"It was just a few guys handing out posters," wasn't so bad.
They'd convince me to forget. They'd lure me back to sleep.
They don't know our stories
      I beg:
Shake me awake.

I thought I was done grieving after the vigils, the singing. It'd been two years since the massacre in Pittsburgh. But that summer day made my bruises throb, my scabs pop open—still raw from the last time a man in this city pointed a gun at people I knew.

This is my fear. I whisper on my therapist's sofa with my legs curled against my chest.

No longer just my ancestors' panic. These stories have happened in my lifetime.

For the fifth time I tell my mom about the Nazis in my neighborhood.

I feel the gun rattle in my twisted stomach.

Our fear is now my body.

The coiled potential of finger on trigger opens me wide. The summer gets hotter and every city is burning. I wander the streets, chanting in protest, but the waking dreams of my ghosts overcome me so I can hardly stand. Each threat of the alt-right showing up at a protest makes me sick. My bones tremble with my ancestors' stories. Our stories. The ones from our many lifetimes.

I crouch in the bushes at the end of my street, talking to my therapist on the phone. I ask her how my friends can face off against armed alt-righters without being as scared as me.

"I'm just realizing that not everyone comes from a lineage of murdered people," I want to cry but the tears never come. "It's not normal for a majority of your ancestors to have been killed."

"You're right," she says quietly, letting me sit with the twisted shape of my old, old body.

Later that summer I walk into the urgent care.

"I'm having a heart attack," I whisper to the nurse who walks me down the long, sterile hall. I lie on the exam table, my chest heaving with the weight of hundreds of years. She attaches me to a beeping machine, smiling, amused at the healthy 26-year-old in a paper gown claiming to be close to death. She waits and watches the monitor.

"You're fine," she says with reserved laughter. I run my hand over my pulsing heart wishing she could see the ways my body was under attack.

I write a prayer.
For all who have awoken from the dream.
For the anti-fascists who have always fought inside me and around me.
For myself because I am getting used to this quiet dance of finger on trigger, coiled potential, stepping forward, backward, waiting for a man with a gun to give birth to my future.
I ask the ancestors: give me your pain. Let my spine hold the rushing floods we have lived through. Let my throat turn our whispers into screams.
I want my yelling mouth to wake our people from our dreaming.
So we can finally remember
the fight, and the path
        to get home
to the synagogue   in Squirrel Hill
the trees   in Lithuania
the cemetery   in Klimentov
        my body right here.

All of the homes they have taken from me.
All of the homes I will dwell in again.

Come Back to the Trees

We take you back to the trees in a waking dream.

Curled hands clutch cloves of garlic. A black shawl is tied tightly under an old woman's gaunt and wrinkled chin. She stands on the dirt road in front of a black wooden house. Laughing, she shakes the bulbs in her hand towards me. The roots swing like stiff braids of tangled hair. Her gesture tells a joke I can no longer remember. But I laugh like my bones still carry the humor of fresh and trembling roots.

How do we retell the stories of ghosts?

"We actually lived there by those lakes, my child." They want me to know this. A tall boy points his finger out over the water.

"That's where we caught the fish." I see the animals flopping on the pier. Their bodies are slimy and smooth, not like the shimmering scales I see in cartoons.

"We used huge nets," he tells me. "Woven, braided ropes."

They can see I am crying. I've been sitting on this pier for years, waiting for them. Crying over all that was taken from us.

I look up at their faces to try and find comfort, but they just look down at me, their lips pursed.

These are my ancestors in the town of Vishay.

"What can we say?" the woman holds her hands open in front of her. They are wide, thick and lined. But empty.

"And it was beautiful," a little girl walks up. "I can show you the beauty too."

She takes my hand and lifts me from where I am sitting. I tower over her. She is a child but she guides me down the pier, onto the banks of the lake. There are small, paved roads. And a forest of birch trees to our right.

"Through here is where we tell stories," she giggles. Not like the deep laughter of the old woman, but a flurry of excited joy.

"I'm glad you've come back here." She looks over her shoulder at me and squeezes my hand, pulling me along.

We wander deeper into the forest, but I can only see images from the YouTube videos I've watched of these trees. In them tour guides walk along paved roads through Vishay's nature preserve. They smile up at me from a shaky 2012 camcorder.

"Really, try to come back with me," she says seriously. She snaps her fingers and the paved roads of 2012 dissolve. We stand on a floor of twisting roots and fallen pine needles. The trees are tall and shiver in the blowing wind.

"This is the forest of my world," the girl says, taking me farther and farther into the past.

The forest stretches out as a great expanse.

There is an old woman with a sunken face far down the path. She bends over to pick something up from the ground. A yellow kerchief covers her head and is tied under her chin. She chews on her toothless gums.

"Ask her why she's here," the girl prods me.

"Why are you here?" I ask.

"Stay with her," the girl encourages, knowing I am doubting. Knowing I am slipping into the present, running back to Pittsburgh.

"Why are you here?" I ask again, staying with this woman in the yellow kerchief.

"To build the little houses."

I bend down on my knees to see what she is doing. There is a small house at the base of the tree. The woman opens the door and my body lurches forward as if it is picked up by a gust of wind. I start to panic. The door gets closer and reveals a deep darkness inside the tree's trunk. We are swept inside the massive tree.

The little girl looks at me and smiles reassuringly.

"We are part of the trees," she explains.

"Like our name," I whisper. Bereznitsky, my family's name before coming to America. It meant birch tree.

The girl nods.

"And the story of my great uncle who talked to the trees as he returned to Vishay after the war."

We lean against the inside of the tree and feel its warmth wrap around us. It seems to expand to hold us. The girl puts her hands behind her head and leans back comfortably.

"It feels so homey in here," I say.

"It is," she whispers. With a sudden flash of golden green, her eyes illuminate. I flinch with fear.

"Don't be scared," she smiles, and starts to move up the inside of the dark tree. She sighs and with her breath dissolves into the bark. I watch her in disbelief. She was next to me and then suddenly she was gone. I hear her laughter radiating from the wooded trunk surrounding me.

"Try it, come with me!" her voice echoes from inside this massive, living creature.

I lean back, not believing any of this to be possible. But I dissolve into the bark just like she had.

We become the tree. And I notice the forest from inside the trunk.

We sway and tremble in the winds, we smile when the old woman comes to build houses at our base, and we laugh when the kids dance and sing around our roots.

One day I hold her hand, trembling. Bad things have been happening in the village and we've heard screams from miles away.

"Move!" we hear a man yell, followed by many feet crunching over the pine needles.

We watch as soldiers lead men, women, and children through the forest. They are crying and screaming. They stop right in front of our tree.

We hear gunshots and watch the bodies of these once living people fall to the ground.

We sob.

I look out from my place in the tree with puffy red eyes and startle; there are shimmering figures hanging above the dead bodies.

"What are those?" I ask fearfully.

"Those are souls," the girl tells me. "You can see them now."

The spirits hover over their former bodies. The forest has slowly consumed the bones and skin that once made a person. But, for decades now, these souls have been unable to return to their source and find rest.

"Show them how to find peace," the girl asks me.

We rush out of the tree and approach the wailing, wandering ghosts.

"Come with us," we say. They sob in our arms. We bring the souls to the trees. We show them the little doors and they open them curiously. With the same ferocity as I had experienced, they are swept into the trunks. They have as much fear and panic as I once had, but slowly they relax. Safe inside the tree, we bring them coffee and listen to their stories.

"You can rest now," we say. They cry on our shoulders. We let them wail for as long as they need.

When they're ready, we teach them how to dissolve into the massive trunk.

"Lean back. Relax. Don't be scared."

They accept that it is time to change; it is time to be calm, to sway in the breeze and find home in these forests.

And they do. We become one—us and the souls and the tree. Together we watch the Earth grow and change. We smile at the warmth of home.

Together and one—us and the souls and the land that we loved. Finally. Not running or fearing anymore. We remember each other again.

Sometimes we still leave the sanctuary of the tree. The girl and I love to rush through the forest. We feel the wind on our cheeks, splash in the glistening waters, and watch light fall through the green leaves. This is our home.

"It is yours, too."

I am back on the bank of the lake. Wind blows through my hair and my feet dangle over the water. I am sitting on the dock and my ancestors surround me.

"I want to come back home, but they've made us so scared," I say.

The little girl takes my chin in her hand. I look up at her and she transforms into an old woman.

"This is your home, your forest, your lake. These people stole it from us," she throws my face back. I hear my family's nets splash against the ripples. I look to the shore and watch barely dressed children dive into the sloshing waters, and rush back to the shade of thin branches.

"Wake up," she screams. "Remember where you are from. Remember your home."

"But the ache," I scream. "My body aches and I can't remember anything."

I realize: this whole time I was the one forgetting the ancestors, the village, the way the land knew us. I was choosing to stamp out the memories so I wouldn't have to feel the pain of longing for such an imperfect home.

"They said we couldn't come back here. You don't have to live with that," I scream at the old woman who lived and died in this village. "This has always been your home."

"You're right," she says. "I don't know what it feels like to try to return to a land that has already released me."

She pulls me into her skirt and holds me. I wail and she comforts me like I am a dead soul she is calling back to the trees.

She strokes my hair and calmly says, "All I know is this world is meant to scare you. But we must return to ourselves. To our homes. The Earth depends on this. You can do it."

She walks off.

I sit on the dock in my ancestor's village.

In this waking dream, the land remembers my name.

A Sunset Over a Lake

We drove into Vishay.

My sister and I, we drove into Vishay.

We drove into Vishay and the sun was setting.

The sun was setting over the lakes. The twin lakes. With the bridge cutting it in two.

The water was yellow and red and purple because it was reflecting the sky as the sun set on an August day in Vishay, Lithuania.

The sun set over the lakes in Vishay and we stood on the bridge as the sky deepened its warm colors.

Frogs croaked and hopped over our feet. We bent down to catch them but they jumped through our fingers. The water lapped quietly against the reeds along the shore. The stars rose slowly over the lake. We were here. In the town where my great grandparents, great uncle, and all of their ancestors had lived.

Mir zaynen doe.

My sister and I stood on the bridge watching the sunset in Vishay.

Our new cousins, the Breznitskys, stood on the bridge with us. When my great grandparents fled Vishay they left behind their siblings—the great grandparents of these cousins. The family tree split on this bridge, 100 years ago. And now the Leventhals and Berznitskys stood on the bridge in Vishay watching the moon grow and glimmer in the ripples of our great-grandparent's lake.

The sun set and the sky became blue with a dusky darkness. Grasshoppers chirped in the trees. We wandered toward the raucous noise of content insects on a summer night. Our older cousin, Ilya, stared at a giant map of Vishay and its forested paths. He looked at it and mumbled in Lithuanian, pressing his finger against the outlines of trails and roads.

"Our family's blacksmith shop is down this way," he declared in his thickly accented English. "My father always told me it was at the edge of the shtetl, right down here."

He took off and we followed him along the forest path, into the shadows of tree branches that were inviting us in to find our home.

I looked up from our walking and could no longer see Ilya. He had run so far into the darkness he had disappeared.

"He does that," his son Danas laughed. "He runs ahead, stays behind. He moves at his own pace."

The sun had set over Vishay and we walked on the wooden path that wound through the forest. Breznitskys and Leventhals, in the forest of Vishay.

What does a family, so long separated, speak about?

We talked about the trees.

"My grandfather left Lithuania for Israel in the 90s," Ioana told me. "He came back once to visit and he stood right here, in this forest, and cried. I asked him why he was crying and he said he had missed these trees so much. 'There is nothing else like the trees in Lithuania.'"

I wanted to cry, too. I stared up at the dark silhouettes of trunks and branches. I was in the forest of Vishay at last. I had missed these trees so much. But I stayed quiet. How could I explain to my new family how I longed for a place I had never been? A place they had visited as children. Their grandparents and fathers had taken them back to Vishay on the yartzheits' of our ancestors. They had shown them the paths and the lakes.

But I had walked through these forests, too, on Google Maps and YouTube. I'd spent hours traveling through this village. On Wikipedia I had studied the plants and animals that lived here. I could recognize the European tree frogs and purple wild orchids which web pages told me lived only in this region. I smiled at the jumping creatures and fragile flowers I had come to know from afar.

And here were the birch trees. They dotted the entrance of the town, the edge of the bridge, and the winding dark forest. I knew them, too. Through dreams, whispers, and the memories of ghosts. I put my hand on their trunks and rested my face against their white bark. Here were the birch trees who guided me back.

I had longed for such an imperfectly beautiful home: a sunset paint-ing a lake with its warm colors, frogs that darted across paths, green oval leaves that hung from the branches of birch trees.

My cousins knew this country's forests with their wild mushrooms and plump berries. But they, too, had not been born in Vishay. They were born in Vilnius, and some had since emigrated to Israel and Bel-gium and then back to Vilnius again.

"There was nothing left for us here," Danas explained, gesturing with his hands out towards the shtetl.

We were all learning how to return.

It was night time in Vishay and we walked the path to our family's blacksmith shop.

We turned the corner and saw Ilya sitting on a bench. The path ended here, letting out onto a wide dock, jutting into the water, sur-rounded by tall reeds and the croaking of frogs. But I couldn't see a blacksmith shop.

"I must have gotten it wrong," Ilya said, his legs crossed, looking confused.

"It's ok," we assured him. We were all uncertain whether we would find anything here at all. So we wandered to the end of the dock and watched the dark, calm waters. I took photos of our new cousins at the place where our blacksmith shop wasn't.

"It's ok," I assured myself.

A group of Lithuanian teenagers walked onto the dock and Ilya started chatting with them.

"He will talk to them for so long," Danas joked as he wrung his hands and peered over at his father.

We laughed and tried to catch the European tree frogs who ran by.

After some time, Ilya came up to us. The teenagers left, walking down the path we just traveled.

"What did you say to them?" I asked

"I was telling them who I was. But they don't remember me. This new generation doesn't know who I am anymore." He put his head down and rubbed his hands on his shorts.

Ilya's father, Shachne, took him here as a boy. Shanchne was my grandmother's cousin, though they never met. He was born in Vishay and survived WWII by joining the Russian army. He later moved to

Vilnius where Ilya was born. Ilya became a prolific animator, creating art about Vishay and the lives Jews once had in this country.

"This new generation doesn't remember me at all."

We wandered back down the forested path, into the shadows of the tall birch trees.

Dancing in Berlin

Earlier in the summer, I am in Berlin. It is 3 am and I am dancing in only my underwear, sneakers, and a KN95. I am sweating; it's so hot in this club and there's so many people packed next to me. I focus on the pounding techno music. The bass beats against my bare chest and I put my hand on my sternum to better feel the vibration.

I want to stay in my body. Because when I look up I see the grand-children of Nazis dancing around me.

"We're here for a fun time," I remind myself.

I am in Berlin for two weeks to visit my dear friend Elias. They moved here last summer, drawn to the city for its queer culture and anarchist organizing. One by one, my friends from Pittsburgh traveled to see them in their new home. A year later, I am finally ready to visit.

I am dancing in my red underwear, my hand on my chest. My friends are smiling, trying to hold onto the beat and each other as the music gets faster. I come close to Elias's partner and yell in her ear so she'll hear me.

"You seem so grounded. I keep looking at you so I don't float away into my mind."

She laughs, "I don't feel present at all! I'm looking at you to not get lost in my thoughts."

I shake my head and smile. The rhythm of the club ebbs and flows with the DJ, the drugs, the sun slowly rising.

Exhausted, I move to the bench by the side of the dance floor and sit, putting my head between my knees. I don't want to look up. If I do, I know I will see my ancestors screaming. They are here too, urging me to leave. To put my clothes on when I am around the grand-children of my enemies.

My chest heaves from dancing and I watch my sweat drip down my nose, making small puddles on the floor.

"Ami!" a friend calls out to me. I look up and they wave at me. But I stop focusing on the beat of the music, my sweating body. So I see my ancestors' ghosts. They are crying, hovering above the heads of the dancing people.

I startle and remind myself I am here for a good time.

But they are screaming.

"Their grandparents killed us!"

It is hard to ignore them.

"Look!" They yell, as I watch the ghosts of the blonde Germans appear. They glimmer in a translucent blue light. I watch the ethereal scene of the ghosts siccing dogs on my people, and making them work in the sun until they sweat. They strip my people down to their underwear and then I have to look away.

This scene plays out above the heads of the dancing people who have glitter on their cheeks and fanny packs slung around their naked waists. We are the children and grandchildren of this tragedy.

Today, we dance. We gather for a fun time.

I move back towards the music where I see my friend Anna. She is tall and has a long ponytail that swishes behind her as she moves.

"Want to go up to the front?" I yell.

"For sure," she responds in her British accent.

We push past the rows of looming cis men gathered by the DJ stand.

"The music feels so good," I shout into her ear. She nods vigorously and sways her hips, smiling to herself. Everyone faces the DJ, eyes closed or just partially open. We all dance in small movements, rocking, shaking. We push ourselves into a collective trance in this dark room. Our sweat pours from our bodies and the low base beats our hearts.

This party becomes a temple for our healing.

You killed my ancestors.

And now we are dancing. Our sweaty, nearly naked bodies tremble next to one another. We see our ancestors' ghosts and do not ignore their stories.

In the dark of the club, we allow our ancestors to see us too.

I tell my German friend about my time dancing and they laugh.

"Oh you are really having the classic Berlin time, theorizing about the club scene."

I know I am playing the trope of the Jew who comes to Berlin to heal their pain. But I am also coming to Berlin to see how the Germans are healing. I want to know if they were ever 19, drinking too much and holding onto toilet seats while yelling, "Can you believe this happened? Can you believe this happened?"

I ask a German anti-facist if he ever screams in open fields when the pain becomes too intolerable.

"How are you healing?"

His eyes widen and he starts to smile.

"We don't ask ourselves that question," he says slowly. "Germany has less of a focus on healing than on being good and restoring ourselves as good."

So it is 4am and I am dancing with Anna at the front of the club. We are in a packed room, surrounded by Germans and hundreds of people from all over the world. Every weekend in this city, lines curl around the outside of looming buildings with throngs of people waiting to enter these pulsing, dark spaces.

Why do they come in such large numbers?

The rhythmic music pulls me deep into my mind. Everything quiets. My ancestors stop screaming. In the tranquility of my slowly moving body and the steady techno beats, tears fall from my eyes, mixing with my sweat.

"It's ok to grieve," they whisper. "It's ok to dance."

I wonder if the Germans hear the voices of my ancestors here, too.

Lovers, Companions

When I first arrived in Berlin, Elias picked me up from the airport. "I'm standing by a gold-plated car in the middle of the airport?" I texted them as I watched groups of people gather around the tricked out car.

There were tired travelers like me, exiting the airport, weary with bags in their hands. Forming next to us was a crowd of others who had seemingly arrived just to look at this car. I couldn't understand what people were excitedly saying about this oddly placed automobile. The German consonants crushed together into combinations of sounds I had never heard before. Among the mumbled conversations were words here and there I could recognize from my basic Yiddish, but they were sparse.

"Found you!" Elias shouted as they threw their arms around my shoulders. I leaned into their hug. We found each other again in this strange land.

A day after I arrived, we took the train to Elias's friend Anna's house. When we got out of the station, I rested my back against a linden tree on the side of the road and started to cry.

"We're gonna be at Anna's house soon, Ami," Elias told me, trying to help me regain my composure.

"I was just so, so lonely," I cried. "I had to leave."

"I know," they held me and I buried my face in their shoulder.

I was crying about Pittsburgh. Maybe for the first time or the last time or the hundredth time. Before I came to Berlin I had moved out of that small city in the hills, into my parents' house in Silver Spring. It had all become too much: I was worn out from carrying so much pain from the communities I was in. Too many Nazis in my neighborhood.

And I missed my friends, the ones who had moved and the ones who were still there but I didn't see as often anymore.

I was becoming too much: I needed a lot. The longer I stayed, the more difficult it was to feel cared for.

It was hard to remember when the hurt from Pittsburgh began and ended, but I knew it was time to let go.

"Come on," Elias said, gently taking my hand and guiding me down the sidewalk.

Later that week I walked with Selmar through The Feld, a giant airport that activists converted into an open park in 2010. Throughout, there were winding gardens dotted with handmade platforms to climb and lie on.

We sat under an arbor of branches covered in thick, twisting grapevines, and watched the sun get lower in the sky. Selmar, Elias's friend, was German. Under the grapes they told me about contemporary fascist activity in Berlin and the conservative party in the south called the Christian Social Party. The conservatism surprised me. More Nazis in the neighborhood. But I'd heard for years how much Germany had changed since the 40s.

"Let's catch the sunset," I said, and we got up and started walking down the old tarmac landing strip. Rollerbladers zoomed past us while couples sat on blankets watching the sky change colors.

I told Selmar the ways my people still hurt because of their people.

"But Germans must be in pain too," I said as we cut through an outcropping of trees planted in man-made dunes. "It's traumatizing to be the perpetrators of so much violence."

I'd never actually talked to a German about any of this. Selmar and I self-consciously laughed at the cliche of a Jew and a German calmly discussing the Holocaust as the sun set over us. We were the poster children for the contemporary vision of the German state, and simultaneously our respective ancestors' greatest fear.

"I just know there is so much silence about it in our own families," Selmar explained. "We learn what the Germans did in general, but everyone assumes their family wasn't part of it."

I wanted to forgive this reaction,
> *who can carry the weight of such violence?*
and take revenge because of it,

who can choose not to carry the weight of such violence?

Mostly, I just felt tired of carrying the weight of such violence.

But the contradictions were ok. I was sharing my story with someone who had as much stake in this tragedy as I did. I had learned that inflicting violence on someone was an intimate act; it entangled perpetrator and victim forever. Rather than remaining passing people, a moment of brutality entwined the strangers' histories and futures. Three generations later, Germans and Jews were still dancing in the reverberations of so many fingers on triggers—still unable to escape this disturbing partnership, constantly building an identity that relied on the motion of the other.

When the sun had set, Selmar walked me to the train station and wrote down a string of letters that I couldn't pronounce.

"That's the stop you get off at," they explained.

I took the train back to Elias's collective house where I was staying. When I got there I stood in front of the mirror in my room. I stared intently at my reddish-brown hair, squinting my almond-shaped eyes at my newly flat chest. I looked beautiful, older, stronger.

I wrote in my journal, "There is something about releasing anger and pain—or at least letting someone else carry the pain with you—that changes you internally and externally."

A week later Selmar and I kissed on their roof as the sun set over the Berlin skyline.

"We keep finding each other at sunset," I said, thinking of all the times in Judaism when we start prayers or holy days as the twilight rolls in. In each other's company, we were becoming aware of this sacred time.

We made our way to their room and I noticed a book on their shelf I had just read.

"Belonging?" I pointed at the title of the book. It's about a German woman who traced her family's history during World War II.

"Yes! It's so good, what did you think about it?" they asked me.

But I didn't want to talk about World War II anymore.

I leaned over and kissed them instead.

"What if Selmar and I are both tokenizing each other?" I asked Elias as we walked along the crowded canal in Kreuzberg, trying to avoid a sudden deluge of rain. We ducked under an apartment overhang and huddled together with other pockets of people who were speaking in German.

I was starting to grasp more of the German conversations around me. The brief moments of clarity left me with an insatiable desire to join in with my Yiddish. But even though I was beginning to understand, whenever I spoke people could hardly understand me.

One afternoon at the kebab shop down the street, I paid for my sandwich and the man working behind the counter thanked me.

"Danke schön," he said to me.

"Sheynem dank," I replied, and he looked at me with confused eyes.

The German around me was a reminder of the old language that was thick on my tongue. The misalignment of comprehension and speech made me want to speak Yiddish even more. But I couldn't find anyone to speak to. I felt like a ghost trying to communicate but not being heard by the people standing right next to me.

"Just see what happens. I doubt things with you and Selmar are just about your identities," I stopped focusing on the conversations around me to hear Elias's reply.

We watched more people running out of the rain until the once filled canal walk was deserted.

A few days later, Anna drove her car out of Berlin with Fiona—Elias's partner—and me in the backseat. We were going into the German countryside to camp by a lake. Elias, Selmar, and their partner, Cam, were joining us later that day.

We drove past flat fields lined with trees in perfect rows. There were forests in the distance, dotted with uniformly spaced pines. The further we drove out of the city, the more my body started to reverberate with old, old fear.

Were there ghosts here too? I asked a naïve question, hoping the trees could just stay beautiful.

The meandering fields reminded me of Pittsburgh's rural countryside during the summer. Before Elias left for Berlin, we drove to a camping site in the Laurel Highlands for a last trip together. Tulip trees and eastern hemlocks tangled together along rushing, rocklined rivers. Every summer the moss filled paths, and big blue lakes, beckoned us to play.

"I'm going to miss you," I had said to Elias after months of trying to convince myself that I wouldn't. I had stared ahead at the road, trying not to look at them.

"I'm not going to disappear," they had put their hand on mine.

"But I'm scared to be here without you."

Scattered amongst the sugar maples and pawpaws was lawn after lawn strewn with Trump signs, echoing the voices of angry ghosts from so many generations.

"Jesus is my savior, Trump is my president."

"This is Ultra-Maga Country."

These angry ghosts had come to animate angry, living bodies; and they had wanted me to feel like I didn't belong there. And still, the trees and the rivers had called us to come play. So we had listened and drove deeper through the red, red countryside.

In Berlin with Anna and Fiona, we pulled off at a small grocery store to buy food for the weekend.

"I'll buy veg, you buy snacks, and Ami you can get fruit," Anna said, texting Fiona and me a list of food.

I walked into the grocery store and started gathering grapes. I could feel my bones vibrating with a panic that was unplaceable. I didn't belong here. The German letters on food packages that I had been starting to sound out became totally unrecognizable. The conversations of the blonde Germans around me reverted to a flurry of indecipherable, crushing constants.

"I need to get out of here," I said to Anna, a dizziness creeping into my vision, a tightness crushing my chest so it was hard to breathe.

I walked quickly outside to the parking lot and paced along a small strip of green lawn. My eyes began adjusting to the tiny details of the landscape; snail shells hanging on blades of grass, pinecones nestled near the curb. The Earth started returning to me.

My phone buzzed from Elias, "We'll see you soon? You good?"

I held a snail shell in my hand, running my finger along its spiral. The simple shape welcomed me in.

The campsite was a wide open field on a hill above a lake. People camped close to one another and gathered around bonfires at night, reminding me of scenes from Renaissance faires. Stars filled the sky and we laid on our backs, trying to see them all.

During the day I wandered down to the lake and perched on a stump overlooking the water. Naked German children with blonde hair dove into the sloshing waters and then ran back to the banks, crouching and eating blueberries. Their naked parents taught them how to point their hands above their heads and break through the water's surface without making any splash. The sun filtered through green and yellow leaves, casting shadows on the sandy shore. It was beautiful.

And I wanted to cry; for all of my longing:

> A lake
>
> A language
>
> Ancestors who could teach me how to dive into water just so
>
> A home.

Selmar walked up to me and put their hand on my shoulder. I leaned into their touch as I kept staring out at the water.

"I realized Germans have pain from what happened," I said to them, swallowing back tears. "But you still have the land and the language and the customs to help you heal." I watched the kids so comfortably swim out to the dock in the middle of the lake. "It is different."

"It is," Selmar said, nodding their head as if they had always known this definitive difference even as I had tried to find congruence in our experiences.

These lands still knew their name.

The sun was about to set and Elias and I held hands, walking down a long, wooded path into the former Ravensbruck Concentration Camp for asocial women and girls. The camp was next to the site where we had spent the weekend, and Elias's friends wanted to visit before we left the area. We entered this concentration camp that so many other women, queers, and trans people never left. I felt Elias's hand grip mine tighter as we took in each other's "asocial" trans bodies.

"I love you," I whispered to them and kissed their cheek with the enduring care of a lover turned companion.

"I love you, too," they said back.

We walked through the camp as dusk was coming. Selmar and Cam moved along the history placards created by local anarcha-feminists while Elias, Fiona, and Anna listened to a self-paced audio tour.

But I kept getting dizzy. There were so many ghosts of girls who wanted to talk.

They crowded around me, trying to get my attention.

"I can't understand you," I whispered to them, lying. I knew their language, but I didn't want to know what they were saying. I couldn't hold the depth of the pain they carried.

I sat down on a garden bench and tried to focus on sorting snail shells by color and then shape and then color again.

"You ok?" Selmar walked up to me and put their hand on my shoulder.

"Mhm!" I lied again, holding a shell between my fingers.

I felt like I was going to throw up. I knew if I stopped focusing on the sorting, the ghosts would keep trying to talk to me in a language I could understand.

The self-guided tour finished and the sun had fully set, filling the camp with an eerie, inky darkness. Everyone was debating who would ride in which car or take the train back to the city. I kept sorting snail shells.

"The last train to Berlin leaves in 20 minutes!" Selmar looked at their phone with alarm. "Cam and I are going to take the train, we have to go."

"Come on," Elias grabbed my hand. Startled and in a sudden rush, we hurried down the wooded path towards the entrance. Shadows of trees and darkened brambles blurred around us as we ran, leaving behind the ghosts of the girls like us.

Selmar nervously packed their bags into the car as my eyes adjusted to the glow of headlights. We gathered around the automobile as people talked frantically about who was going where, bags in their hands. I looked around, the girls were gone.

Selmar came up to me and smiled, waving their hand. I reached out to them and hugged them, pulling them tight against me so I could rest in their arms for a moment. Our reverberating dance of so many generations was slowing down. I wanted to feel the stillness between us at the gate of the camp.

An engine began to hum.

"Bye." They kissed my cheek and pulled away from the embrace.

They got into the car headed to the train station. It was the last time I saw them.

Elias and I held hands and watched stars fill the wide, beautiful sky.

A clock rings twice a day in the middle of Munich

"I didn't know I was still allowed to feel so sad about what happened." We walked down the cobblestone street in Munich. Castle-like walls towered over our winding path. The chimes of the city's 1908 glockenspiel clock rang out behind us.

"I didn't know I was allowed to either," I said, my throat catching on my words.

Her grandparents survived concentration camps and she didn't know she was still allowed to feel so sad.

We passed by the German tourists. They drank pitchers of beer and smiled up at the ringing glockenspiel clock. Every day at 11:00 am and 12:00 pm the clock's 43 bells toll, sending 32 tiny wooden dancers spinning around the clock's hands, enacting scenes of theatrical romance and revenge. Boisterous crowds fill the square to watch the giddy performance.

The charming show takes place just a few feet from the Old Town Hall where a small plaque remembers. At that location in 1938, Joseph Goebbels gave the infamous speech that incited Kristallnacht. All over the country, Germans had smashed in synagogues and Jewish shops and homes, so everywhere the streets were filled with shattered glass from my peoples' buildings.

"Hasn't it been too long since it happened for me to still be so affected by it?" the young woman asked while the Germans gathered to remember the time. The tourists raised drinks to their lips, I pushed back tears.

Almost

Ilya walked us through Vishay. He was looking for the small cottage his friend wanted to sell him for five thousand dollars.

"I think it's over here," he said as he checked his two cell phones for the address.

It was sunny but cool. Lila and I walked down the road next to the lake, imagining the life that existed behind the cottages' lace curtains. We dreamt up summer time tables filled with potato cepilinis and bowls overflowing with fresh raspberries. In the winter we'd build warm fires in the wood burning stoves while drinking cups of hot lindent tea. We'd pass time, waiting for the ground to thaw enough to begin our spring vegetable gardens.

"I'll call my friend again, I can't find the house now," Ilya announced as we stood next to a big open field.

"We'll take a break," Danas assured his father.

Danas told us our relatives used to gather for holiday celebrations on this big field. We sat down under a tall tree where kids now played soccer a few yards away. Lila closed her eyes. A family pushed their baby in a stroller along the paved path in front of us.

Ilya leaned against his grandson, David, alternating between nodding off to sleep and checking his phone for the elusive address of the home for sale in Vishay.

"Could you imagine coming back here in the summers?" Danas asked me.

"Maybe, I think I could."

"We'd buy the house, fix it up. Then every summer the family could come and get back together here."

"That'd be amazing," I said. "I like it here. You?"

"I do," Danas said. Then slowly he shook his head and laughed. He picked at the grass, disturbing a cricket who jumped over his finger. "The only problem is that all of the neighbors are the descendants of people who killed our family."

But it was so beautiful: The big inviting lake and the tall birch trees. We used the map I had found on shtetllinks.com to find what remained. My great-grandfather's house, number 66. It was next to the grocery store where people said hi to one another while they bought frozen cepilinis and pints of sour cream. Cars drove over the bridge by my great-grandmother's house, number 62, which still stood next to the former synagogue. It looked like our family had left just a few weeks ago. Doors locked for a long vacation, waiting for us to come back.

How could there be any problems? When the remnants of our families' life were all still there in Vishay, Lithuania.

But here we stood,
outside
of the buildings
without a key.

We walked up to my great-grandfather's house with its blacksmithed metalwork. It was made of light colored bricks with a sky blue vestibule sheltering the front door. Lila pushed her nose against the windows. The new owners had turned the house into an auto parts store. Work tables and boxes of car accessories now filled the bottom floor. A man walked up from the road and Ilya started talking to him in excited Lithuanian.

"It's the guy who owns the house now!" Ilya translated.

"Can you ask him if we can go inside?" I pushed.

"He says maybe tomorrow, if he comes back while we're here."

But he never came back.

My great-grandmother's house was next to the synagogue. Its yellow paint was chipping and a collection of satellite dishes crowded the roof. We walked along the fenced yard, watching a family water their garden, unload groceries from their car, make lunch for young children. A small surveillance camera was mounted on the doorframe of the house, watching us back.

We noticed each other but no one said anything. I asked Ilya if he could introduce us but he seemed to not hear the question. Were we invisible to these people in our great-grandmother's home? Or were we so visible they didn't want to admit who we were?

We wandered a few feet to the synagogue that was now a Baptist church. Here, my family had davvened three times a day. They'd gathered in these walls for weddings, klezmer performances, Purim spiels. Here, my ancestors had been locked up by Nazis before they were killed.

The building was painted a darker shade of green than I'd seen in the pictures online. It was huge and loomed over the lake. Beautiful lace curtains hung on the windows. We walked around each side, trying to find an open door, but every entrance remained locked.

I remembered from the video on YouTube that there was once a plaque on the outside wall declaring that the church was formally a synagogue. But I couldn't find the plaque; it had since been removed. It was now just a tall, green church that we had no way of entering.

Earlier in the summer, when I was in Berlin, I went on a tour of the State Department as part of a trip for American Jewish young adults. We spoke to one person there: the director for the Office of the Special Officer for Relations to Jewish Organizations, Questions on Anti Semitism, International Affairs of Sinti and Roma, Holocaust Remembrance. She was responsible for helping Jews with German ancestry restore their German citizenship and property rights. She spoke with such clarity and assurance about how her role was to restore Germany as good.

At the end of her speech she asked if we had any questions. I could feel the reverberations of so many ancestors vibrate through my chest.

"Ask her about us!" they whispered to me. "Ask her about our homes!"

I raised my hand and wondered again where courage comes from. But I did it because my ancestor's had not been able to stand before this woman while they were alive.

"Yes?" she pointed at me with her manicured finger.

"I feel so much sadness and longing for the lands my ancestors came from."

The corner of her mouth twitched.

"I want them back," I said. "There's a cemetery in Klimentov, Poland and a synagogue in Vishay, Lithuania. Our family lost them for good during the Nazi Occupation. Can you help me get them back?"

The room went quiet. I wasn't supposed to know about these lands that once knew my name. I should have learned how to forget. The Jews were safe far, far away. The Germans were adamant about supporting Israel. There were monuments all over Germany to remember what happened. Germany was doing good now. I was supposed to be happy.

She took a breath.

"Thank you for your question," she said, nodding her head. "Unfortunately that is under the jurisdiction of the Polish and Lithuanian governments, and we can't interfere in issues of foreign property acquisition." She smiled, content that she'd given the right answer.

My ancestors' screams tore through my body.

On our last day in Vishay we tried to find the Jewish cemetery in the shtetl. Ilya remembered it being one place, and Danas somewhere else. It was hot and we tried in vain to fan ourselves. As we searched for it, we passed the Christian cemetery. Its graves were crowded together into a gated piece of land in the center of the village. Fresh flowers adorned each one.

"I think it's over here," David said. He sprinted away, running towards a hillside in the distance.

We followed slowly, finally catching up to the young teenager. He stood in front of a rusted chain-link fence. The gate was unlocked and we entered.

There, a wide field opened in front of us. A short dirt path led to a stone marker adorned with lanterns and small rocks. A plaque on the large stone was engraved with a Jewish star and Yiddish writing, "Der Alter Yidishe Beit Olam," "The Old Jewish house of the Afterlife."

The gate to this home was open, the dirt path welcomed us in.

"This is the cemetery," I said.

Behind the marker was a grove of trees. Peeking out of the trimmed grass were gravestones inscribed in Yiddish and Hebrew. As we walked closer to the trees, we saw more graves. They were nestled next to tall trunks and tucked against protruding roots.

We pushed deeper into the cemetery. Ilya and David ran ahead, weaving between tree trunks and jumping over fallen branches. Lila walked behind them, stopping every few moments to take pictures of the graves. Mushrooms grew out of logs and David held up a massive bloom, startled by its large size. More and more graves appeared and the trees grew denser and denser. Soon, we were standing in a thicket of ivy, roots, and headstones.

The sun dappled through the branches, dousing us in dreamy golden light.

"The trees have been caring for our dead while we've been gone," Lila said.

"It's so beautiful," I said, leaning over the graves marked with our ancestors' names.

Later that night, Lila and I sat on the dock in our ancestor's village. We were still outside our great-grandmother's house and the synagogue. But from here, we could watch the water lap at the reeds at the edge of the bank. I breathed out and lay back on the platform.

"I can't believe we're here," Lila said.

"I know."

In the quiet I could hear the crickets chirping and the tree frogs beginning to croak.

In that waking moment, the land remembered my name.

The Fruit of Rotting Trees

Surrounding the shtetl was a forest of birches and pines and other trees I didn't recognize. We walked through the woods to get to the swimming lake, and every few steps my cousins would step off the path and wander to a fallen log or an old tree stump. Squatting down, they'd run their hand over the bark, peeling back the rotting wood to reveal blooms of mushrooms. Taking out knives, they'd cut back the fungi and place them into their backpacks.

"We'll cook them up tonight," they told us. My sister, Lila, and I were weary; we'd never eaten wild mushrooms before and we were flooded with panicked thoughts of a poisonous death in a foreign land.

But my cousins knew which mushrooms you could eat.

"We just grow up learning that in Lithuania," they explained.

Danas told my sister and I about hiking in America. It was the height of mushroom season and all along the path were huge, prized mushrooms, late in their growing season. Common foragers in Lithuania would have harvested the treasures within days of their blooming.

"In the US, most people don't realize the good mushrooms they're walking past." Danas had spent that afternoon gathering the overlooked fungi from the American forest.

That night, for nearly two hours, Ilya stood at the sink in the kitchen, his back to the rest of the room. He was barefoot, wearing a sweat-stained white linen shirt. Next to him was the huge pile of mushrooms, collected from the forest that morning. He held each mushroom under cool, runningwater, carefully washing the dirt off of each fold in their caps. With a small paring knife, he deftly cut off pieces of the tough, soil encrusted stems.

It was almost 11:00 p.m. and we hadn't started cooking the mushrooms yet. We'd already eaten a tomato salad, pickles, and dense, meat-filled czepilinis. Ilya slipped out from the table and left for nearly twenty minutes to go to the car. We weren't sure where he had wandered to in all of that time but he returned holding black rye bread and a can of salmon caviar.

"A special treat!" he announced, peeling off the metal tab on the tin of fish eggs.

The youngest cousin, David, grew too tired and walked upstairs to bed. Danas passed around the chocolates he brought from Belgium and poured us small glasses of Lithuanian beer. Ilya returned to the sink to keep washing the mushrooms.

Danas walked over to his dad. "Alright, it's good enough, let's cook them."

"Ok, ok," Ilya put his hands up in jest and surrendered the mushrooms to his son.

Danas pulled out a tub of sour cream from the fridge.

"We throw them in a pan with some oil, a bit of parsley, lots of sour cream," Danas showed my sister and me. The mushrooms began to sizzle when they were put on the heat and they turned a grayish-white in the thick cream. The room filled with a dense, savory smell.

In a few minutes Danas carried over a plate for each of us. Each dish was piled with an amount of mushrooms I could not have afforded to buy in the US. I stared at the bounty, grinning.

"Well, you going to eat it?" Danas smirked, digging his fork into the food.

I smiled and took a bite, filling my mouth with the deep, nutty flavor of the fruit that grows from the forest's rotting trees.

Two months later, in October, I was in Baltimore with my younger sibling, Naomi, who hadn't gone to Lithuania with us. It was their birthday and they had just taken me to the Baltimore mushroom festival. We'd spent the day in the forests surrounding Baltimore, listening to speakers present about mushroom philosophies and drinking shiitake tea. At the end of the day an experienced forager took us into the woods to look for mushrooms we could harvest.

We walked through the forest as the guide pointed out the large, wet, dying branches that made good homes for mushrooms.

"The key to mushroom hunting is to search one small area deeply, rather than covering a wider area less carefully," she instructed us as she sent us off to forage for ourselves.

Naomi and I walked to a fallen tree trunk by a dried up creek. Crouching down, Naomi ran their hand over the bark.

"Look!" they exclaimed, pointing to blooms of translucent oyster mushrooms. They gently pulled at the stems and collected the fragile mushrooms into a container.

Later that night I was in the kitchen cooking spiced rice for Naomi and their friends.

"Are we going to eat the mushrooms?" I asked Naomi.

"Yeah, of course." They took the collection of mushrooms from that evening and dumped them into a pile next to the sink. Barefoot, they took a mushroom in their hand and held it under the cool, running water. Seemingly practiced at this, they gently scrubbed the dirt from the folds of the mushroom caps.

I watched them and noticed how much they appeared like Ilya that day in Lithuania. Both hunched over the sink, letting dirt wash down their fingertips, into the drain.

Naomi turned back to look at me, their blue eyes locking with mine.

"I'm having so much deja vu," they said.

They brushed their fingers against the mushrooms' smooth gills. I was nearly waiting for them to take a jar of sour cream out of the fridge and for the nutty, savory scent from the kitchen in Lithuania to fill the room.

Our bodies remember the fruit from such old, rotting trees.

"Come home"

My sister and I run off the dock and jump into the lake in Vishay. Suspended in these waters, I sink down with my eyes closed and my feet floating in front of me.

Above me I can hear the muffled sounds of the Lithuanian children playing. They talk in a sing-song language that only my cousins understand. Their grandparents wade in the shallower waters by the tall reeds and cattails. These old men and women learned how to swim on this lake and they've taken their children and now grandchildren here every summer to do the same.

Fish swim by my toes, their fast movements blowing bubbles against my body. I open my eyes for a moment to watch the small creatures dart around in the clear blue water. Streams of sunlight dance on their gray scales. My sister's legs kick while the fish weave around her.

Earlier, Ilya told me stories about the lake water's healing powers.

"Do you see that old guy over there?" Ilya pointed at the man standing in front of our great grandfather's house. "He's old but he has perfect teeth and few wrinkles because he washes in these waters every day. They'll keep you young and alive forever."

I imagine my great great great grandparents bathing in this lake. Maybe that's how they stayed alive long enough to meet me.

Beneath my ancestors' waters, I can see the faint colors of the tall birch trees surrounding the lake. They look different through the water; their trunks appear like tall, white phantoms, their leaves as long strands of hair dangling from ghostly bodies.

"Hello," I say to the trees. The image of their swaying leaves trembles in the refractions of the rippling surface. "Thank you," I whisper.

I remember the way the trees talked to me years ago. I wrote what they told me before I knew I would be here.

Silver trees sink their roots into the banks of twin lakes. Barely-dressed children dive into sloshing waters then rush back to the shade of thin birch branches. Sun streams through layers of oval leaves, painting yellow and green shadows across dripping, naked bodies. The children crouch and eat blueberries, the trees whisper to the ones who will listen.

"Come home."

I listened to the birches
and I returned:
To the trees
To my body
To my ancestor's ghosts.
And throughout the next year, I will continue to return.

First to New York, walking through the Lower East Side where my great-grandmother wandered barefoot. Pain will course through my feet as my footsteps send the streets' hard cement vibrating through my bones. I will cry for the first time —real, big tears —for all that has happened. And a new lover will hold me in their arms, letting me feel at home for a moment in a city my family once left.

Then to Berlin and Poland. Elias and Fiona will come with me to see what remains of my great-grandmother's cemetery in Klimentov. My fourth cousin will tell us which neighbor to talk to and which towns to avoid on the way. We will stand next to the big white synagogue where the man gathers my family's candlesticks. We will try to see something, anything —and, if we don't, we will still say we had a good time.

In April, I will return to Pittsburgh for three weeks when the trees are budding green and pink on the hillsides and the rivers are shining with what appears to be thousands of jewels. I will return and see the children at Hebrew school who sent me out of the city with the youthful wish that I would follow my dreams. I will hug them and see how tall they've grown in a year. I will hope they still sing and dance like we used to.

And the man who caused me to shatter into thousands of pieces four years before will return too. He will be on trial for murder when I am visiting Pittsburgh. He will make me return again to my grieving, rageful trembling. But no matter what the court decides, my people and I are returning

to the fight we have been waging

for thousands of years.

Under the water, I blow more bubbles from my nose, sinking deeper towards the lake's bottom. I feel myself getting heavier and heavier as the air slowly leaves my body.

I look up, and the water above me breaks open with a crash; a child is curled into a perfect cannonball. They clutch their small arms around their folded legs as they hit the water. A pummel of froth splays out from their body like fireworks. I hear their friends howling in joyful whoops as the child slowly sinks into the white plume of water they churned with their diving.

The ripples around them move with a sudden force, firmly pushing me down, deeper into the lake's depths. I open my mouth in surprise and a rush of water fills my throat, replacing the last bits of air in my lungs.

I'm alone in the lake's waters

and I'm starting to choke.

I kick my feet, rushing to the top of the lake, breaking through next to my sister, coughing so hard I can taste blood in my mouth.

"Are you ok?" Lila holds my shoulders as we tread together.

"Yeah, yeah," I manage to say as I pant and gasp. Water and spit drips down my chin. "It's just so beautiful."

Squinting behind my wet hair, catching my breath, I look out at my young cousin on the dock. He is blowing a strand of tall grass, trying to make it whistle like a cricket's chirping. In bathing suits, Ilya and Danas sit against a tree, eating the blueberries my sister and I bought at a farm stand in Vilnius. They speak in Russian and Lithuanian, with some Yiddish words thrown in. The branches on the silver birch trees sway in the slight breeze. The sun comes through their oval leaves, painting yellow and green shadows on my sister and me.

How did the trees know this would happen, so many years before?

I cough again. More water streams out of my nose, burning my nostrils as it leaves.

"It's so beautiful."

Acknowledgements

I would like to thank the many people who have helped make this book possible. I am grateful to the wisdom and care I have received from the mentors, friends and family members who have supported me throughout this journey.

First, thank you to the Strangers in a Tangled Wilderness collective members. You believed in this book since I sent you the manuscript. Your edits and encouragement have helped me understand the power of my words. Casandra, thank you for interpreting my stories into such beautiful art and illustrations. I never imagined I would actually publish a book and you all helped make this dream a reality.

Thank you to Rabbi Phyllis Berman. You have always encouraged me to be vulnerable and accept the truth of who I am. I would not have the courage to share these stories without you.

Thank you to Cindy Crabb. You have helped me greet both the pain and magic that exist in my body—showing me how I could come home to myself. This book is an outpouring of so much of the healing I have done with you.

Thank you to Cindy Barukh Milstein. You have been there for me in grief and celebration. Wrestling with ideas together helps me imagine that another world could be possible.

Thank you to my friends and mentors who have inspired me and held these stories with me: Ilana, Lena, Vilde Chaya, Corina, Yael, Lexi, Ru, Erin, Jane and Hannah.

Thank you to Jesse, Danas, Ilya, and David for telling me your stories and showing me around your cities and forests.

Thank you to Cat for swimming in summertime lakes with me, watching fireflies and cheering me on.

Thank you to the many, many people involved in Ratzon: Center for Healing and Resistance. Jess and Ben, you two affirmed me and my vision and I am so grateful for all you are continuing to do to grow our queer, Jewish, anarchist community.

Thank you to my Nightshade family: Flip, Leo, Tahel, Tzipora, Elias. You are the backbone of so many of these stories. You have been my rock during these turbulent times. Becoming contenders in the realm of thought with you has been one of the greatest joys of my life.

Thank you to my grandparents, David, Rinky, and Bob. Honoring your memories has opened the door to this work. To Grandma Joyce: Thank you for helping me see my writing as a gift and for loving me unconditionally in such big and small ways. Every moment we share, I wrap with a bow.

Thank you to my family. Naomi, you have always been my creative coconspirator and confidant. I love collaborating with you to make our visions come to life. Lila, you joined me on this journey of ancestral healing and the adventure of returning to our shtetl. I treasure our travels together along with the quiet times we share. My dad, you gave me my first real writer's notebook when I was seven and you have encouraged me to write ever since. You teach me the power of humility, humor, and a curious mind. My mom, thank you for creating such a warm and loving home for me to return to. You have always taught me to speak up and use my voice to stand up for what is right. I am grateful to have such creative, loving and bold people to call family.

And finally, to the ghosts who are still living. Thank you for greeting me and letting me share your stories with others.

I wrote these essays on the ancestral lands of Dionde:gâ: the Seneca language name for the Pittsburgh region. This is the ancestral land of many different Indigenous peoples including the Seneca Nation and members of the Haudenosaunee Confederacy which included the Mohawks, Oneidas, Onondagas, Cayugas, and Senecas. This area was also the home to the Lenape, Shawnee, and others. Genocidal colonizers violently and forcibly removed Indigenous peoples from their ancestral lands here in Dionde:gâ. As I tell these stories of my own family's ancestral pains, I acknowledge my role in continuing the ongoing violence and colonization of the Indigenous peoples of my area.

About the Author

Ami Weintraub (he/they) is a Jewish anarchist writer and Rabbinic student. He has contributed to a number of publications including *Tikkun Magazine*, *Jewish Currents*, and *New Jewish Voices*. Ami is the founder and former director of Ratzon: Center for Healing and Resistance, a Jewish, queer anarchist community center in Pittsburgh and is studying to become a Rabbi in the Aleph Rabbinic Ordination Program. Ami's work and community organizing focus on building a world without domination where people can freely connect to their cultures, lands, and bodies. They call the hills of Pittsburgh, PA and creeks of Silver Spring, MD home.